Self-Care

SELFISH OR SACRED?

*An Interactive Guide to Myths
and Misunderstandings*

Susan L. Fink

ISBN 978-1-63961-221-5 (paperback)
ISBN 978-1-63961-222-2 (digital)

Christian Faith Publishing
832 Park Avenue
Meadville, PA 16335
www.christianfaithpublishing.com

Printed in the United States of America

CONTENTS

FOREWORD

While reading an early draft of this book, several lines stopped me. Here is the first. The author writes, "For ten years I worked as a director of volunteers for a hospice program. My prayer was that my words and actions would reflect Christ's light."

From experience, I know that Susan's words and actions regularly reflect the light of our Savior. My heart was touched when I read how she prays for this. But the above is not what stopped me cold. Let me explain before sharing those words.

My friend's brother had cancer, and he lived in the same city as Sue. Knowing that Sue worked in hospice care, I called her for help. Could she give me information and advice? Susan offered much more. In fact, it was later that I found out Sue had visited the man, a person totally unknown to her except that he was sick and in need. The man's sister, Deb, told me the story with unabashed thankfulness over the unexpected, kind gesture that had offered her dying brother comfort and hope in Jesus.

Now for the words that stunned me the most. Frustrating her to tears, Susan admits that her work with hospice care had mentally and emotionally drained her until, as she writes, "the LORD rescued me." For ten years she had suffered because of an unhealthy employment environment. Yet her experience had enabled her to be there for Deb's brother. Because she cared. Because she was moved by the love of Christ to serve.

Sue's unselfishness made a difference in more lives than one. She surely served the patient. But she also served Deb and their entire family. She served her Lord. Little did any of us realize at the time that even within an aggravating situation, God was equipping her.

Susan Fink is a spiritual woman who speaks and acts from her heart. Yet I had no knowledge that turmoil raged inside her for a decade as she cared for others while neglecting her own needs. But as always, our faithful Lord had a plan. He wanted her to write this book. Her heartfelt words are meant for the workaholic and for those suffering from low self-esteem. They are written for people who, like Sue, love their Savior and know their self-worth comes from God. They are written for those entangled in myriad myths and misunderstandings. She will unravel the lies. Readers will identify with Susan's candid admissions as they ponder the difference between self-care and selfish ambition. They are not synonyms. And because we are both saints (in Christ) and sinners, each of us daily faces our own similar but personal dilemmas.

The format is easy to follow. The questions spark conversation whether digested personally or shared with friends. The research, the insights from fellow believers, and the truths of Scriptures will make you think. And the book will warm your heart. Read and enjoy. May this Christian approach to knowing how self-care differs from selfishness make a difference in your outlook. It did for me, and I am grateful that the Lord led this author to share.

Mary I. Schmal

QUIZ

Will this book benefit you? This quiz will determine the answer.
Check which statements describe you:

___ I can relax in a bubble bath or hot tub only if I also have something else to read or do.

___ When brushing my teeth, I walk around the room to locate the next item I need.

___ My work computer is part of my vacation luggage.

___ While enjoying a walk through flower gardens, I think of my to-do list.

___ A vague feeling of guilt hangs over my involvement in games, bonfires, and coffee hours with friends.

___ I do not think it is right to turn down a request for help, even if I know I'll regret doing so.

___ Most often I regard taking "me-time" as selfish and time-wasting.

___ Most, if not all, of my hobbies involve mentoring or including others in the activity.

___ Sometimes when I have helped a person for a sustained period of time without seeing any improvement or appreciation, I am surprised. And then I'm ashamed for feeling resentful.

___ It's much easier to say yes to serve others than to say yes to myself.

___ When I see a need, I can't resist responding, no matter what stress it may involve.

___ I spend so much time making sure house guests are fed and happy, I forget to enjoy their company.

___ If I won a big lottery, chances are I would spend little of it on myself.

___ I'm unable to set assertive boundaries for time-consuming, energy-draining people.

___ Making sure other people enjoy themselves concerns me more than winning a game.

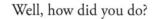

Well, how did you do?

Scoring: If you could identify with any of these statements, the answer is *yes, you need this book.*

The extra spaces and pages in the book are for your journaling, doodling, prayer writing, and other personalization.

The book's format for each chapter first takes a look at the

 myths or misunderstandings about self-care for Christians, shares

 my struggle regarding the chapter's topic, then offers ideas to identify

 your struggle. That chapter section is followed by Scripture-based

 truth and then an illustrative reflection.

 The "Motivation Identification" section contains questions to encourage journaling and sharing.

 A "Summary" section follows as well as suggested

 "Prayer Prompts."

INTRODUCTION

When work on this writing project slowed down to a no-progress mode, my friend (a retired English teacher) asked if she could give me an assignment. Being a people-pleaser I immediately answered, "Sure."

"Write one page today," she encouraged. "Just *one* page."

My brain quickly jumped to my promises and plans for that day: take a church member to the doctor and pharmacy, assist my husband with preschool and Sunday school Thanksgiving projects, call a lonely friend in assisted living, and set up a transportation schedule for my elderly parents.

My thoughts started spiraling. "Sure, I can write one page," I thought to myself. "But that seems so self-serving when all these other opportunities seem more significant, or at least more spiritual. Dare I prioritize a project I want to do? Wait a minute! What am I writing about? Guess I do have trouble giving myself permission (or a needful, strong kick) to write about that!"

If you (like me) tend to forget what self-care involves and excludes, my prayer is this study will provide convicting encouragement in God's will for your life.

CHRISTIANS AGREE ON THE DEFINITION OF SELF-CARE

MYTH OR MISUNDERSTANDING

Have you ever heard or agreed with any of the following beliefs?

- Scripture condemns self-care when it says, "Do nothing out of selfish ambition or empty conceit" (Philippians 2:3).
- Most people care too much about themselves.
- Self-care is an excuse for more "me-time," which stems from prideful self-reliance.
- My annual medical checkup is my self-care, that's all I need.
- We should be focusing on Jesus, not self-help.
- I am blessed with good health. So I don't need to do any self-care.
- The self-improvement industry makes lots of money with gimmicks appealing to vanity.
- My parents demonstrated self-sacrifice, a strong work ethic, and the value of achievement at all costs. I strive to continue what they taught.

For some Christians, using the term *self-care* makes them feel uncomfortable. They rightfully quote Mark 10:18, "No one is good except one—God," and Psalm 16:2, "You are my Lord. I have no good apart from you," to clarify value comes only from Christ. We don't need to care for ourselves, they conclude, because God fully supplies our "every need, according to his glorious riches in Christ Jesus" (Philippians 4:19).

Does this mean when we are overwhelmed, hungry, and tired (like Elijah in 1 Kings 19), we can expect angel intervention?

Other believers suggest Jesus's admonition to "take up your cross, and follow me" (Matthew 16:24) means denying any attention or pleasure to self. However, the Greek translation of this quote indicates identifying with Christ, being ready to suffer for the gospel truth if need be.

The definitions of self-care and self-esteem are easily transposed. Author Don Matzat contrasted the latter term to "Christ-esteem" in his book *Where the Search for Self-esteem Ends*. Matzat wrote about finding purpose and confidence in Christ to overcome insecurities. The book emphasizes putting our worth in God's hands to stop striving, worrying, and wondering if we are enough. Believers don't need to seek higher "self-esteem" because "God raised us up with Christ and seated us with him in the heavenly realms" (Ephesians 2:6). We are defined by Jesus's righteousness, not by our sin. At the same time, we do have stewardship responsibilities while living in our "earthly tent" (2 Corinthians 5:1). Being aware of our many needs does not prompt self-reliance, but humility.

> Humility is not thinking less of yourself,
> but thinking of yourself less. (C. S. Lewis)

> Above all else, guard your heart carefully,
> because your life flows from it. (Proverbs 4:23)

MY STRUGGLE

Pastors have assured me the "love your neighbor as yourself" (Matthew 22:39) passage is an encouragement to love ourselves, as well as our neighbor. But dare we assume everyone understands what this entails? Counselors will tell you self-hate keeps their offices very busy. If not modeled by mentors, where do people learn proper self-respect and love? Personally, I am still learning the how and why.

Some Christians, like me, are prone to view themselves through the lens of the law more than the gospel.[1] Often, the Holy Spirit rightfully reminds me of my eternal distance from God's perfection: my sinful nature. But sometimes my mind confuses guilt (disobe-

---

[1] Because God is perfect in his holiness and justice, all people need to be rescued from their ungodliness (sin). Jesus humbled himself to live on earth for thirty-three years as God/man. He perfectly fulfilled the law's requirements of obedience and sacrifice. The gospel is the wonderful news of God's forgiveness, love, and peace with him, through Jesus's life and death on a cross in our place. "In the gospel a righteousness from God is revealed by faith" (Romans 1:17).

dience) with shame (despair over who I am). The self-torment of inadequacy and inferiority are feelings Satan uses when we forget our worthiness in Christ. Also, it is easy to misunderstand the definition of self-love. This term is not what Timothy is condemning when he writes, "People will be lovers of themselves" because he further defines these same individuals as "without self-control, savage, haters of what is good" (2 Timothy 3:1–3).

As God's chosen child, I am no longer under the old covenant of "If you keep my commandments, then I will bless you" (1 Kings 3:14). Do you know people who feel they can't be forgiven? I have moments like that until I allow *facts* to overrule my *feelings*. The truth is, when God looks at me under the new covenant of grace, he sees Jesus—who fulfilled that law.

> Jesus loves us in spite of ourselves, loves us so much that he died to cleanse us of the guilt our self-centered love has brought upon us. It is the dynamic that gives purpose and meaning to our lives. (Kenneth Kremer, *For One Another: Touching Hearts in a Changing World*)

> Do not be afraid, because I have redeemed you. I have called you by name. You are mine. (Isaiah 43:1)

> For he (Christ) himself is our peace…by setting aside in his flesh the law with its commands and regulations. (Ephesians 2:15–15 NIV)

YOUR STRUGGLE

Are you tempted to say "Yeah, but" as you analyze your worth or need for self-respect? Since the start of time, humanity has continually messed up, ignoring the pursuit of God's will. Despite all that, Christ's followers are wholly redeemed, restored to a perfect relationship with their heavenly judge. Because Jesus made us loveable, we disrespect his work when we neglect to love and care for ourselves.

Do you intentionally create space (or margins) in your life for emotional energy, relationships, laughter, and joy? If not, what beliefs or excuses are preventing you from valuing your well-being?

> "Look at the birds of the air. They do not sow or reap or gather into barns, and yet your heavenly Father feeds them. Are you not worth much more than they?" (Matthew 6:26).

Recall how the Creator purposely designed men and women in his image as the highlight of all creation (Genesis 1). Also, if King David regarded his body "fearfully and wonderfully made" (Psalm 139:14), why do we hesitate to honor ours? Because every sinner was "bought at a price," the grateful Christian's response is to "glorify God with your body" (1 Corinthians 6:20). Would that not include loving care for your mental, physical, relational, and spiritual well-being?

> To be sure, no one has ever hated his own body, but nourishes and cherishes it, just as Christ does the church. (Ephesians 5:29)

> Could we say the things which we consider self-care are actually the means by which God cares for us? To rest in him is to express faith that he provides food, rest, medical care, etc. And it also demonstrates a humility that knows God is welcome to enlist other people to do his work (aka ask for help!). (Leah Alair)

TRUTH

 "A person who lacks self-control is like a broken-down city without a wall" (Proverbs 25:28).

House buyers are wise to hire experts to check the home's foundation. The basement is an especially important place to look for wall cracks, uneven floors, sagging support beams, or a leaning chimney. God-given responsibilities, opportunities, our health, as well as relationships with others, are building blocks for our temporal life. Self-care is a vital foundation for our earthly existence.

Caring for our well-being to better enable productivity for God's purposes is a part of sanctification.[2] The Holy Spirit works to separate his children from temptations and sin, enabling faith to grow and produce fruit. One goal of self-care is to "not let sin reign in your mortal body...but rather...offer every part of yourself to him as an instrument of righteousness" (Romans 6:12–13).

The promise of "Seek first the kingdom of God and his righteousness, and all these things will be given to you" (Matthew 6:33) is not condemning self-provision, but is an encouragement to exclude worry. A well-known tactic of the devil, worry distracts us from blessings, causing us to doubt how "all things work together for the good of those who love God" (Roman 8:28).

Satan also uses discouragement and despair to convince us we are not worthy of doing God's will. Scripture affirms the powerful, reliable resources for each aspect of life—our Savior's Rx for mind, body, and soul.

We are not called to bury our strengths, cower in comparison, or sit immobilized in self-

---

[2] Justification refers to the saving work of Jesus who has paid for our "just-as-if-I'd-never-sinned" status. Sanctification is how we live as Christians, relying on the Holy Spirit to guide our behavior, thoughts, and desires. Through the use of the Word and sacraments, God gives and grows faith and fruit our daily life. This sets us apart (sanctifies) as God's chosen.

doubt…(but) be eager vessels built for his purpose and capable of moving mountains. (Jes Woller, author of *Miraculous Debut*)

REFLECTION

My grandmother's veil-covered wedding hat is on display in my home. Because of its value to me, it sits safely behind glass doors on a high shelf. When Christians value the Lord's Supper, they don't carelessly grab the wafer or drink the cup in a nonchalant way. And pastors don't use the water and the Word haphazardly during a baptism. Do you toss your Bible, thus respect for God's Holy Word, on top of the trash? Just as we treat treasured and holy things with reverence and respect, shouldn't we do the same for our body and soul where the Holy Spirit resides?

Author and blogger Sara Borgstede calls fitness an act of worship. She encourages readers to put forth their best effort (2 Timothy 4:7) and set aside any worry about performance (Luke 12:22–23) in pursuing physical health. She also advises planning for spiritual nurture.

Which of Sara's self-care habits (listed below) do you currently do? If you were convinced of the long-term benefits of investing in wellness, which activities could you make a commitment to do?

- Journaling, prayer, and Bible reading time every day
- Eating healthy, wholesome foods
- Starting an exercise habit
- Doing a relaxing activity, such as reading a book
- Getting enough sleep
- Planning time into my week for my spouse and kids
- Working hard at my job but not overworking
- (Taken from theholymess.com)

Note: I don't know about you, but the older I become, the more I feel a need for rejuvenation. Since these recommended activities promise a personal revival, I am on board!

Caution: Any adjustment will feel awkward or uncomfortable at first. Perhaps pick just one activity to start. Most often it takes ninety days for something new to become a habit.

> I take joy in the process of caring for my body not only because it is an incredible gift from my Creator, but because it was bought at a price on the cross. (Elisa Gross, Kingdom Workers, Chile Program Coordinator)

> Prayer, time in the Word, sleep, and fellowship with other Christian women—these things tend to recharge me. (Amber Albee Swenson, author)

MOTIVATION IDENTIFICATION

Journal your answers and/or discuss with a friend or group.

1. I AM MOTIVATED TO CARE FOR MYSELF BECAUSE IT AFFECTS MY OUTWARD APPEARANCE.

2.   I PURSUE SELF-CARE BECAUSE I BELONG TO GOD.

3.   THERE ARE THINGS INVOLVED IN SELF-CARE THAT PUSH ME OUT OF MY COMFORT ZONE, FOR EXAMPLE:

4.   WHAT WOULD ASSIST ME IN EVALUATING MY SELF-NUR-TURE NEEDS?

5.   WHEN MIGHT I HAVE A TENDENCY TO VIEW MYSELF UNDER THE LENS OF THE LAW?

SUMMARY: SELF-CARE OR SELFISH?

When some believers think about *self*, they rightly identify with Paul's confession: "I fail to do the good I want to do. Instead, the evil I do not want to do, that is what I keep doing" (Romans 7:9). Paul is referring here to the struggles of our inner sinner and the Holy Spirit within us at the same time. In Romans, he assures there is no condemnation for those in Christ and how "those who live in accordance with the Spirit have their minds set on what the Spirit desires"(8:5).

Self-care can be easily misunderstood as "Christ-less self-centeredness." Making my wants and needs first in every situation is idolatry. Would the term *self-care* sound more biblical if *self-control*, a fruit of faith, was used in its place?

In Titus, Paul writes how God's grace "trains us to reject ungodliness and worldly lusts and to live self-controlled, upright, and godly lives" (2:12). The Lord also encourages us to "run with patient endurance the race that is laid out for us" (Hebrews 12:1) by exercising self-control in all matters (1 Corinthians 9:24–25).

> "Add moral excellence to your faith. To moral excellence, add knowledge. To knowledge, add self-control" (2 Peter 1:5–6).

This book's definition of self-care includes treating our God-designed body, mind, and soul with reverence. We are, after all, his loved and forgiven children. Because our bodies are members of Christ (1 Corinthians 6:13, 15) we strive to be good stewards, not ignoring our multidimensional physical and spiritual needs.

My growling, empty stomach and dry mouth do an expert job of alerting me to my body's cravings. From Eden's garden to wilderness manna, feeding hungry crowds, healing the sick, and granting us daily bread, our heavenly Father demonstrates he knows, cares, and provides for our physical needs.

Jesus points out spiritual needs when he said, "Blessed are those who hunger and thirst for righteousness for they will be filled"

(Matthew 5:6). This promise refers to receiving soul-satisfying blessings. The Holy Spirit prompts us to humbly realize our soul's dehydration. He provides the continual living water (John 4) to cure our spiritual thirst. Believers are blessed with spiritual refreshment through the Lord's Supper and hope-giving renewal through his Word. Christians are spirit-enabled to love and care for others and themselves when they see Christ within.

> To anyone who is thirsty, I will give freely from the spring of the water of life. (Revelation 21:6)

> Self-care is a tension to manage, not a quick solution. (Pastor Mike Novotny)

PRAYER PROMPT

Ask your loving heavenly Father to help you honor him by honoring all he created. Thank him for the wonderful way he made your body, soul, and mind.

Your prayer space:

SELF-CARE IS NOT FOUND IN THE BIBLE

MYTH OR MISUNDERSTANDING

To be a Berean (see Acts 17:11) is an encouragement to dig into the Bible and make sure what is being taught is found there. This has been a wise discipline for Christians through the ages. Part of the miracle of Scripture is how the simplest of minds can grasp and trust "Jesus loves me" and yet lifelong study continues to reveal and inspire more knowledge. The Holy Spirit enables faith growth as we learn from authors and preachers who know the Bible's original languages, "correctly handling the word of truth" (2 Timothy 2:15).

One of many God-given gifts is reason. We use it when comparing Scripture with other parts of Scripture, a cardinal rule of accurate interpretation. But when or if our human reasoning hits a wall, God's Word trumps any logic. After all, if I could figure out in my tiny brain everything about God, he would definitely not be big enough to create and sustain the vast universe! Nor would he be worthy of worship!

In connection with this book's topic, does Paul's "in humility consider one another better than yourselves" (Philippians 2:3) contradict Jesus's instruction to "Love your neighbor as well as you love yourself" (Matthew 22:39, *The Message*)? The passage "each man will bear his own burdens" (Galatians 6:5) denotes there are some burdens we should not carry for others but is each person's responsibility. *Burdens* would include caring for personal daily needs, especially our relationship with our Lord.

> When we honor the way God made our bodies and brains, respecting our need for space, recovery, sleep, nutrition, etc. we have more energy and often longevity to serve people with our lives. (Pastor Mike Novotny)

MY STRUGGLE

Somewhere in my young adult years, I learned (or assumed) caring for others' needs should always come before mine. One example was when my teacher preparation classes properly emphasized doing what is best for the students. I observed (and still know) excellent, caring instructors who dedicate most of their waking efforts to school-related tasks. And why wouldn't they, especially working at a Christian school where ultimately God is your boss? It often seems an expected sacrifice for energetic teachers to neglect their health and social needs or postpone them until summer break.

Now, as a retired, vintage person, I struggle to care for myself without feeling prideful and self-absorbed. I need to remember, however, when my basic human needs aren't met, my focus will eventually turn to my emptiness. Love can't be drawn from a depleted well. If there is no self-maintenance plan, I'm more likely to respond sinfully in stressful circumstances. When physically, emotionally, or spiritually malnourished, I lack self-discipline and faith-fueled joy.

There is a business in my hometown with the sign "Preplanning Center." I drove past it many times before realizing it was a funeral home. Being proactive about our funeral choices and expenses takes a difficult responsibility off our loved ones. Shouldn't we also be prudently planning for our daily needs while on this side of heaven?

YOUR STRUGGLE

Have you invested money in a retirement account? It takes discipline to save money for the future. Has the Lord given you a talent in the arts, teaching, technology, or other skills? Are we discrediting him when we don't acknowledge those gifts? Self-care allows unrushed time to practice, improve, and use those talents. Investing in yourself shows gratitude to the One who calls you redeemed and precious.

Do you struggle to acknowledge it is virtuous to invest in yourself?

TRUTH

At the end of his life, Jesus prayed to his Father, "I have glorified you on earth by finishing the work you gave me to do" (John 17:4). How could our Savior claim completion when he did not help, heal, or preach to everyone?[3]

In his earth-bound humility, there were times Jesus addressed his own weariness by telling the crowds to leave so he could go up onto the mountain by himself to pray. And sadly, when he asked for support during his heart-wrenching Gethsemane prayer, the disciples were "not able to stay awake" (Matthew 26:40).

> "Jesus came to serve, yet there are times when he left sick people sick, lame people lame, etc., as he took time for himself or said to the apostles, 'Get into the boat. We need some us-time.' He had compassion on the crowd and yet didn't feel guilt about getting away from them" (Pastor Mike Novotny).

Those who think self-care is akin to selfishness, point to directives such as: "When arrogance comes, shame follows, but with humility comes wisdom" (Proverbs 11:2) and "Humble yourselves in the sight of the Lord, and he will lift you up" (James 4:10). But is the humility God asks of us anti-care, self-hate, or something else?

---

[3] Jesus even said no to a city full (possibly thousands of people) wanting him to come and heal them (Mark 1:32–38).

The core of the gospel message is Christ's sacrificial love for all. When he tells us to "love your enemies and pray for those who persecute you," it implies mercy for all, including ourselves.

God not only tells us to pray for our persecutors and provisions but he also encourages, "Keep asking…seeking…knocking, and it will be opened for you" (Matthew 7:7). Prayer is a sacred privilege and a necessity for soul care. "At every opportunity, pray in the Spirit with every kind of prayer and petition" (Ephesians 6:18).

Paul gives detailed directions regarding assertive soul care in Ephesians 6:13–17, "Take up the full armor of God, so that you will be able to take a stand…with the belt of truth buckled around your waist, with the breastplate of righteousness fastened in place, and with the readiness that comes from the gospel of peace tied to your feet like sandals. At all times hold up the shield of faith, with which you will be able to extinguish all the flaming arrows of the Evil One. Also take the helmet of salvation and the sword of the Spirit, which is the word of God." These defensive and offensive pieces of tactical equipment protect and strengthen the wearer.

MOTIVATION IDENTIFICATION

Discuss or journal your reactions.

1. WHEN I PLAN FOR MY SELF-CARE, I FEEL AN EXAGGERATED SENSE OF SELF-IMPORTANCE.

2.   MY FAITH AND MINISTRY GROW WHEN MY BASIC HUMAN NEEDS ARE NOT IGNORED BUT TAKEN CARE OF.

3.   WHAT DOES THIS QUOTE MEAN TO YOU? "HUMILITY IS NOT THINKING LESS OF YOURSELF, IT'S THINK OF YOURSELF LESS" (C. S. LEWIS).

4.   WHAT DID YOUR HEAVENLY FATHER SACRIFICE FOR AN ETERNAL, INTIMATE RELATIONSHIP WITH YOU?

SUMMARY: JESUS DEMONSTRATED SELF-CARE

Paul emphasizes a Christlike servant attitude that acknowledges, "It is God who is working in you, both to will and to work, for the sake of his good pleasure" (Philippians 2:13). We can trust the Lord's promises to "give rest to everyone who is weary" (Jeremiah 31:25). As Creator who humbly took on human form, he understands our requirements for respite.

> "Come to me all you who are weary and burdened, and I will give you rest" (Matthew 11:28).

When his sister berated him for not going back to China as a missionary, Olympic runner Eric Liddell responded, "God made me fast. And when I run, I feel His pleasure." We can know God's pleasure when we persistently nourish our souls with his Word. When we strive to correctly handle his truth, praying for wisdom in personal application, God approves (2 Timothy 2:15).[4] We were lovingly created to care for the earth, our amazing bodies, and fellow humans. In doing so, we glorify the Creator.

> Let your light shine in people's presence, so that they may see your good works and glorify your Father who is in heaven. (Matthew 5:16)

> God from the very origin of creation has established a principal and a pattern by which life works. All work and no rest doesn't simply make Jack a dull boy but makes him a sad and futile creature. No, no, says the writer (of Hebrews 4:10–11), it's the very rhythmic cycle upon which humanity has been ordered, and we

---

4 "Do your best to present yourself to God as one approved, a worker who does not need to be ashamed and who correctly handles the word of truth."

have deviated from it to our great distress and discomfort. (Alistair Begg)

We cannot give our hearts to God and keep our bodies for ourselves. (Elisabeth Elliot)

PRAYER PROMPT

Thank the Lord for the gift of prayer. Ask him for a desire to study Scripture and for wisdom to understand differences between pride and humility, selfishness and self-care.
Your prayer space:

THERE IS LITTLE DIFFERENCE BETWEEN SECULAR AND CHRISTIAN VIEWS OF SELF-CARE

MYTH OR MISUNDERSTANDING

"To thine own self be true: thou canst not then be false to any man" (*Hamlet*).

A critical difference between secular philosophy and Christian belief has to do with sources of worth or value. Secularists pursue and find purpose through temporary achievements such as appearance, productivity, relationships, intelligence, status, and employment.

One popular theory is Abraham Maslow's *hierarchy of needs*. According to this psychologist, a child's self-esteem can be realized only after his psychological, safety, and love/belonging needs are met. At the peak of this hierarchy is *self-actualization*: "The achievement of one's full potential through creativity, independence, spontaneity and a grasp of the real world" (dictionary.com). This perspective includes focusing on a person's strengths, seeing differences in human nature as valid alternatives, and being responsible for one's own happiness. Supposedly, self-actualized people "accept themselves and others (and are)...able to enjoy themselves and their lives free of guilt" (Talevich et al., *Toward a Comprehensive Taxonomy of Human Motives*).

Often, those who deny the existence of a Creator think they have autonomous power to do whatever they want with their bodies and minds. "My body, my choice" is the cry of confused people who don't acknowledge biological facts. Conversely, prolife advocates promote the sanctity of *all* life, from conception until natural death, no matter what stage, abilities, or challenges.

Bible-believing Christians are taught to treat their and others' bodies with reverence because the "body is a temple of the Holy Spirit...you are not your own, for you were bought at a price" (1 Corinthians 16:19–20). When we disrespect or ignore our body's needs, we are guilty of defiling God's "made in his image" creation.

In many cultures, altruism attempts to mix religious traditions (such as unselfishness) with secular worldviews. This practice most often involves equal concern for people, animals, and the environment. An example of altruism includes celebrities who anonymously donate to their favorite "earth-friendly" charities.

Is it possible for a person who does not know Christ's example of ultimate self-sacrifice to be generous without selfish motivation? Many claim this as their truth, but the probability is debated even among agnostic philosophers.

MY STRUGGLE

Although I have been a Christian for more than sixty-seven years, there are some promises in Scripture that I struggle to apply to myself.

One is, how can my holy heavenly Father label me his work of art when I am a rebellious prideful person? When Paul writes in his letter to the Ephesians (2:10), "We are God's workmanship," the last word is *poiema* in Greek, taken from a verb form of "to make." The New Living Translation uses the term *masterpiece* here. How can the One who sees all my faults call me his masterpiece?

Hanging in my living room are two framed pastel landscapes, one painted by a dear friend and the other by my deceased grandmother. I value them not only for their beauty but because of who created them. Just as I appreciate and care for these works of art, I need to humbly respect the Lord's property—me. Self-care includes self-respect because *God don't make no junk*. He creates masterpieces.

 ## YOUR STRUGGLE

Can you relate to this illustration?

Experience has taught me that I nearly always get sick when I'm run down. So, I don't feel guilt taking steps to preserve my health, but will feel it exposing Christmas brunch guests to my wretched cold. When I'm weak and run down it's hard to seek the good of my neighbor (and I'd probably resent him and feel sorry for myself)! Staying healthy simplifies life. Then I'm liberated to do the work God gives me to do. I'm humbled and honored every time he allows me to run with his torch, and I need to be ready. (Janis Lonnquist Klebig)

Because the Holy Spirit has chosen to dwell within Christians, shouldn't his vessels be conscientiously cared for? Might pride be involved when we place our instant gratification desires above guidelines of healthy eating? Are we missing out on blessings when we ignore our body's needs for exercise and other wellness habits? If you are feeling sluggish or defeated, can you be effective for Christ's purposes?

In our do-what-feels-good, tolerate-all-lifestyles culture, self-denial is unpopular and sometimes unheard of. I know I need God-directed clarity for responsible self-maintenance. How about you?

Make me walk in your truth and teach me,
because you are the God who saves me. (Psalm 25:5)

TRUTH

 Psychological egoism teaches all human behavior is ultimately motivated by self-interest. This is readily observed when toddlers quickly master the use and meaning of "No" and "Mine!"

From infancy to adult, no one has to be taught how to develop a me-first attitude. Theologians use the term original (inherited) sin to describe this. And this is where a Christ follower's motivation makes a defining difference. Do we seek to boost our ego through our own accomplishments, or bow in awe of what our Savior has accomplished for us? Are we filling our empty hearts with various distractions and addictions, or are they overflowing with the Holy Spirit's faith-strengthening power?

> And do not get drunk on wine, which causes you to lose control. Instead, be filled with the Spirit. (Ephesians 5:18)

> Therefore rid yourselves of all evil, all deceit, hypocrisy, jealousy, and all slander. Like newborn babies, crave the pure milk of the word so that by it you may grow up with the result being salvation. Certainly you have tasted that the Lord is good! (1 Peter 2:1–3)

REFLECTION

You have probably heard sermons, attended Bible classes, and read articles that reflected scriptural admonitions to "remain true to the Lord with devoted hearts" (Acts 11:23). Believers gather together to "be mutually encouraged by each other's faith" (Romans 1:12) and "by being rooted and built up in him… overflow in faith with thanksgiving" (Colossians 2:6–7). According to Psalm 1, a person has a fruitful and prosperous life when his joy comes from an ongoing study of the "teaching of the Lord." Another blessing is to "be transformed by the renewal of your mind, so that you test and approve what is the will of God" (Romans 12:2). Continued growth in Bible knowledge is clearly worth all efforts.

How do you actively nourish your faith? Have you discovered the best methods for you to listen, learn, and retain God's truths? Do you underline your Bible with color-coded highlighters, take sermon notes, review Bible study through discussion, or other active learning techniques?[5] Check with your pastor(s) and church leaders

---

5 Visual Faith Ministry teaches creative, interactive ways to prayer, make "sermon doodles" and simple drawings to engage your left brain as you learn God's Word.

for recommended resources such as audio podcasts, devotionals (that can be read or listened to), and zoom-type Scripture studies for your phone or computer.[6] A Bible with a wide margin encourages personal note-taking or adding illustrations to reflect the text. Websites such as www.Biblegateway.com provides an abundance of Scripture engagement techniques, as well as a variety of translations and languages for interesting comparisons.

"Read God's Word now as God's Word, without skipping anything. Underline heavily everything about what our Savior has done for us. And if you like, write 'For me' in the margin" (Bo Giertz, *Hammer of God*).

Soul care includes utilizing assertive tactics. "See to it that no one takes you captive through philosophy and empty deceit, which are in accord with human tradition, namely, the basic principles of the world" (Colossians 2:8). God wants us to know how to wield the needle-sharp sword of the Spirit (His Word) as an offensive weapon against evil.[7] Safeguard your spiritual resources (for yourself and your family) through consistent study, prayer, and memorization.

> If any one of you lacks wisdom, let him ask God, who gives it to all without reservation and without finding fault, and it will be given to him. (James 1:5)

> Always be prepared to give an answer to everyone who asks you to give a reason for the hope that is in you. (1 Peter 3:15)

> We do not take the spiritual life seriously if we do not set aside some time to be with God and listen to Him. (Henri Nouwen)

---

[6] This author's recommendations include TimeofGrace.org, WhatAboutJesus.com, https://wels.net/serving-you/christian-life/womens-ministry/, and the YouVersion Bible App.

[7] Ephesians 6:17.

MOTIVATION IDENTIFICATION

Journal and/or discuss your reactions.

1. LIST WHO AND WHAT NOURISHES YOUR BODY, MIND, AND SOUL.

2. WHAT SELF-CARE BEHAVIORS DO YOU CURRENTLY PRACTICE?

3. WHAT MIGHT HELP YOU REMEMBER THE NEED FOR SPIR-ITUAL STEWARDSHIP?

4. WHAT NEW TECHNIQUES OR METHODS TO STUDY SCRIPTURE ARE YOU WILLING TO PURSUE?

SUMMARY: THE CHRISTIAN PERSPECTIVE ACKNOWLEDGES OUR WORTH AND MOTIVATION IN CHRIST

King David, who God praised as a man after his own heart, wrote about the connection between physical and spiritual suffering. When he neglected to confess his sins (against Bathsheba and her husband Uriah), his "bones wasted away." He describes the effects of guilt on his body in Psalm 38:

> There is no wellness in my bones because of my sin,
> because my guilt has gone over my head.
> Like a heavy burden, it is too heavy for me.
> My wounds stink and ooze because of my folly.
> I am drooping. I am completely bent over.
> All day long I go around mourning.
> Even my back burns with pain.
> My whole body is unhealthy.

The Christian perspective of self-care includes admitting our wrongs, gaining forgiveness and strength through Jesus, applying the instructions in the Bible, and asking God and others to keep us accountable.

> Therefore repent and return to have your
> sins wiped out, so that refreshing times may come
> from the presence of the Lord. (Acts 3:19–20)

PRAYER PROMPT

Give praise and thanks to God for choosing to give you faith and purpose. Admit your wrongs to your perfect holy Savior. Then ask and gratefully receive forgiveness through his redemptive sacrifice.

Your prayer space:

SELF-CARE ONLY HONORS SELF

MYTH OR MISUNDERSTANDING

Have you heard or (as I have) echoed these sentiments?

Self-care is part of a new-age, navel-gazing, all-about-me, selfish pampering lifestyle. It is only for rich people who can afford personal chefs, chauffeurs, and mansion chalets.

When a hungry baby cries, do we label it selfish? Research shows if an infant does not make his needs known, it indicates a probable disability or evidence of abandonment.[8] God gave both animal and human little ones the ability to express the food, safety, and attention needed for survival. Isn't it acceptable, then, for God's children of all ages to know and attend to their preservation?

MY STRUGGLE

Even today, when I read the apostle Paul's "Each of you should look not only to your own interests but also to the interests of others," I skim over the first half of the verse (Philippians 2:4). "Also" assumes believers do care for themselves. So why do I often serve others' interests to the point of neglecting myself? Self-care may sound selfish, but it enables me to "be devoted to one another in brotherly love" (Romans 12:10) more effectively. If I make smart decisions regarding upkeep of good physical health, for example, I'm better able to assist the needs/interests of those whom God has placed in my life.

Have you had unreasonable expectations for your personal health resolutions? Exercise is wonderful. But any good thing can be done too much, too soon, resulting in harm or failure. This can lead to reluctance in starting over again, even at a reasonable pace.

When I first learned my arthritic knees and osteopenia would benefit from walking and weight-bearing exercise, I went out. Joining a fitness club, I used all the circuit machines for at least an hour every day and later hopped on a treadmill or stationary bike. My goal of every day full throttle (for a sixty-five-year-old) was almost met—

---

[8] https://www.apa.org/monitor/2014/06/neglect

until my body signaled a major ouch! It was embarrassing for me to limp back to the gym. The following week, my favorite fitness club machine was the rolling massage bed. Pain can be a strong reminder of stupidity!

I now enjoy taking leisurely nature walks and bike rides. These activities renew me with energy and gratitude. Who can deny the masterful designs and beauty of God's creation? I am awed by "his invisible characteristics—his eternal power and divine nature—[that] have been clearly seen since the creation of the world, because they are understood from the things he made" (Romans 1:20).

> "Nature reminds me: in unfurling leaves, nesting birds who have all they need, slow-moving clouds, sunlight, wind, wildflowers and butterflies back from the south. If this is how He orchestrates in nature without my help, how much more is he doing in my life?" (Sarah Haben).

During the COVID-19 quarantines of 2020, negative changes in children's behavior were termed a *nature deficit disorder*. Research[9] reports how access to green spaces, or merely viewing nature scenes, reduces stress for all ages. The Japanese custom of forest bathing (sitting mindfully under trees) claims it increases emotional intelligence, boosts immunity, and improves memory. No wonder God placed the first people in a garden and called it good!

> The heavens tell about the glory of God. The expanse of the sky proclaims the work of his hands. Day after day they pour out speech. Night after night they display knowledge. (Psalm 19:1–2)

---

[9] https://welldoing.org/article/how-green-spaces-reduce-stress and https://www. researchgate.net/publication/282331597_Green_Space_and_Mental_Health_ Pathways_Impacts_and_Gap.

I go for a daily run to take care of what is mine: my health and my family, in thankfulness. (Brandon Steenbock, Staff Minister)

YOUR STRUGGLE

Have you been fortunate to attend a party where refreshments included a bubbling chocolate fountain? Guests use toothpicks to stab their choice of fruit, cheese, or bits of cake to hold under flowing dark brown sweetness. Hmm! It's delicious to see, as well as taste. But guess what happens when the chocolate runs out? Not a sweet experience for those who are last in line.

Have you discovered what you personally need so your reserves of chocolate-like energy can continue to flow? Do you have friends or family members who expect your generous, continuous support, even when you are depleted? How would you rate your consistency to refill yourself versus refreshing others?

It's not so much about balance in life as it is about priorities. I saw how true that was—before and after my dad's passing. When I realized I had choices about how to respond, take action or step back until I knew more what to do, things changed. I began making more decisions and life adjustments with more confidence. (Robin Fry)

I believe God wants us to be good stewards of the bodies we live in while on earth. It requires planning, faithfulness, and a little sacrifice (time and a willingness to get a little uncomfortable). The consequences of poor stewardship of our bodies are very serious—early death, illness, and lack of stamina to carry out the work God's given us. (J. Lonnquist)

TRUTH

If we acknowledge the Creator made us yet we are not faithful stewards of our lives, are we acting "like a foolish man who built his house on sand" (Matthew 7:26)? Then when the winds of worry and storms of sickness come, they can easily destroy our soul's home.

Faith is nurtured by habitual feeding on God's Word for insight and encouragement. Essential spiritual fuel is gained through unrushed, thoughtful meditation with Scripture. Is there anything else we might study that guarantees such blessings?

> Indeed, whatever was written in the past was written for our instruction, so that, through patient endurance and the encouragement of the Scriptures, we would have hope. (Romans 15:4)

> This Book of the Law must never depart from your mouth, and you are to meditate on it day and night, so that you will act faithfully according to everything written in it, because then you will prosper in everything you do, and you will succeed. (Joshua 1:8)

REFLECTION

We are gifted by God with five senses. Do we include sight, smell, touch, taste, and hearing in grateful and mindful care of our bodies?

Use of our senses markedly affects our mood and concentration. Did you know that smell (our olfactory organs) has a direct line to the part of our brain (limbic system) that processes emotion? For example, the scent is so calming that those who work on lavender farms need to take frequent breaks to stay alert! The smell and taste of peppermint or ginger are refreshing stimulants for most people.

Since the average mouth has ten thousand taste buds, it's no wonder we enjoy delicious food.

Martin Luther said, "Music drives away the devil and makes people joyful." Our psychological responses to music can reduce anxiety and pain. Young David's harp playing was used to calm anxious King Saul (1 Samuel 16:14–23). Scripture set to music helps us appreciate, remember, and share God's truths (Colossians 3:16).

Have you ever wondered if God made the fur of our domesticated animals soft so we enjoy petting them? And who isn't amazed when noting the limitless variety of colors found on flowers, birds, underwater creatures, and other natural beauties?

It makes sense! Practicing self-preservation can be as simple and edifying as exposing our five senses to "whatever is lovely" (Philippians 4:8).

How might you add pleasant sensory experiences to your day?

MOTIVATION IDENTIFICATION

Journal and/or discuss your reactions.

1. CAN YOU THINK OF WAYS TO DO SELF-NURTURING ACTIVITIES *WHILE* STRENGTHENING RELIANCE ON GOD?

2. THINK OF EXAMPLES WHEN TAKING CARE OF YOUR NEEDS LED TO BETTER WAYS OF ASSISTING OTHERS.

3. WHAT ARE SOME WAYS WE COULD USE MORE OF OUR SENSES IN WORSHIP?

4. DOES THE PASSAGE "THE LORD LONGS TO BE GRA-CIOUS...TO SHOW YOU COMPASSION" (ISAIAH 30:18) ENCOURAGE YOU TO BE GRACIOUS TO YOURSELF?

SUMMARY: SELF-CARE HONORS OUR DIVINELY DESIGNED BODY

Most often our body miraculously heals itself. A small paper cut starts a complicated series of processes to stop blood flow and close the wound. But there are consequences when protection warnings are ignored. For example, wearing ill-fitting shoes for a mountain hike is not advised, unless you enjoy blisters.

Have you driven a vehicle with a near-empty gas tank or when it ran out of oil? When your tires are low on air and your shocks aren't sufficiently greased, you are in for a rough ride. If your car is not properly maintained, its use is diminished or possibly terminated.

Similarly, ignoring our body's maintenance is costly and sometimes deadly. Our blood pressure, heart rate, and temperature numbers are called *vital signs* for a good reason.

> We don't honor God with our exhaustion, irritability, depression, chronic disease, wasting time, researching quick cures and diets, or living with obesity by stuffing down our feelings—all possible when we neglect these tents we live in. (J. Lonnquist)

> Self-care is fuel for the selfless…made up of all the people, places, things, activities and experiences that support you and lift you up. (Carly Laabs, theparachuteproject.com)

PRAYER PROMPT

If daily prayer is not a habit, add it to your schedule. Ask the Holy Spirit to teach you God-pleasing ways to love him, others, and yourself. List and express gratitude to him for the many ways he has shown love to you.

Your prayer space:

A CHRISTIAN'S OBLIGATION IS TO ALWAYS SERVE OTHERS IN TIMELY, AFFIRMATIVE WAYS

MYTH OR MISUNDERSTANDING

Isn't saying no to requests selfish? Don't we need to be "all things to all people" (1 Corinthians 9:22) and imitate Jesus's submissive humility?[10] Some Bible believers think we are not fully trusting God's provision when we limit opportunities to serve others, no matter what the reason.

Needy people and worthwhile charities surround us. Thanks to worldwide news, modern man has daily oppressive exposure to innumerable tragedies. How can anyone ignore all the sadness?

When believers see a need, aren't they supposed to respond promptly in loving, provisional ways? Moses felt this way, and he literally had millions of people asking him for help. Talk about being a candidate for burnout! God used Jethro (Moses's father-in-law) to teach him how to deal with the needs of so many.

> Moses' father-in-law said to him, "What you are doing is not good. You will certainly wear out both yourself and these people who are with you, for the work is too much for you... Moses listened to his father-in-law and did everything that he had said. Moses chose capable men from all of Israel and made them leaders over the people: officials over thousands, hundreds, fifties, and tens. They judged all the cases of the people initially. They brought the difficult cases to Moses, but every easy case they judged themselves. (Exodus 18:17–26)

> If we are careful not to take on too much, or to compromise on our own needs and priorities, we can make a difference for others and for ourselves at the same time. (Carly Laabs)

---

[10] John 13:3–14, Philippians 2:5–8

> The art of leadership is saying no, not saying yes. (Prime Minister Tony Blair)

MY STRUGGLE

"Could you find and organize volunteers to serve Lent suppers?"

"If we pack your van with my donations and deliver them to the secondhand store, you and I could walk after."

"You enjoy kids. Can you take my three for a couple of hours so I can get caught up?"

Most often, I feel honored when someone asks me for help. To be bluntly honest, my affirmative answer is often not because of Christian commitment, but due to my desire to feel appreciated and purposeful. Seeking validation, I don't want to disappoint anyone by turning down a request. A commitment is made before judging if it fits my schedule or self-care requirements. Then of course it's too embarrassing for me to back out. I'm often willing to risk burning out by saying yes, not wanting God or others to think less of me.

> Your life isn't yours if you always care what other people think. (Unknown)

> So then, as we have opportunity, let us do good to all people, and especially to those who belong to the household of faith. (Galatians 6:10)

When my congregation, pastor, or Christian brother or sister solicits use of my gifts, I recognize it is God-pleasing to serve. Most often I find satisfaction and joy in giving "especially to those who belong to the household of faith." But doesn't the first part of this Galatians passage, "As we have opportunity, let us do good to all people," suggest there may be some inopportune occasions when I don't help out? For example, if I am not trained as a lifeguard, nor have the proper floatation devices, my attempt to save a struggling, drowning person will most likely cause both of us to sink. Years ago when our international student houseguest needed science home-work tutoring, I wisely recommended my husband. Although I am not comfortable admitting I can't help, I need to acknowledge when something surpasses my limitations.

Sadly, no one is immune to sinful motives when making requests of others. Sometimes an assertive no is needed to prevent people from advantage-taking, provide loving correction, or avoid abuse. Our congregation was happy to provide a car, several rent payments, and babysitting for an unchurched single mom. After many months of neglecting to get car insurance (as she had promised) and spending requested cash donations ("for shoes and diapers") on cigarettes and Diet Coke, we promptly restructured our support.

Our compassionate, sinless Lord halted advantage-taking when he angrily overturned the "church activity" tables of corruption at the temple (Matthew 21:12–13). Righteous indignation is also accept-able for his followers.

If we answer affirmatively to every favor asked of us, what are we saying no to? In the example above, my congregation's contribu-tions to the dishonest mom reduced the amount of money gifted to those with legitimate needs. Might turning down a request enable a better yes for a different opportunity? I need to remind myself in either case, assisting or not, to offer a loving response (Ephesians 4:15).

Since Sunday school days I had the impression that the "Martha, Martha" story was simply Jesus criticizing priorities. Jesus probably had a crowd of hungry disciples with him, and Martha wouldn't have been able to merely pop a few frozen pizzas in the oven. This hostess was overwhelmed with many tasks and was aghast her sister, Mary, wasn't helping.

I can relate to Martha when a large group is expected to our home for a meal, and my husband is oblivious to the many prepa-rations. Martha and I wonder why Jesus isn't motivating our loved ones to help us. We want someone to point out, "Hey, look at all the work she is doing. Don't you feel guilty you are not helping?" With his "one thing is needed" reply, the Savior isn't condemning necessary food preparations. He is gently teaching how worries harm our psyche, distracting us from excellent, eternal things (Luke 10:38–42). Attention to Jesus in Word and worship needs to be a priority over daily tasks. In other words, feeding our faith trumps service.

[Jesus] said to them, "Come away by yourselves to a secluded place and rest a while" (Mark 6:31).

YOUR STRUGGLE

Statistics say 20 percent of church volunteers assist in almost every activity a congregation does. It seems the adage "If you want something done, ask a busy person" rings true in churches too.

Are you able to say no to a serving opportunity, within or outside of the church? Do you continue to do tasks you used to enjoy but now dread? Or has your ability or availability to volunteer decreased? It's not only okay to know your limits and move on, it's healthy! Ask yourself if you are in the best position to serve a specific need at this time. Do you know your gifts and strengths well enough to know which jobs are a good fit? Thinking you need to volunteer for something since no one else has stepped up, or because you've always done it before, is not a prescriptive reason. Might you be depriving someone else of an opportunity to serve? Lack of confidence, along with unknown expectations, most often stops people from offering assistance. Could you personally encourage and mentor someone to take your place? There can't be a positive response if you don't ask the question.

[God] wants [us], in the end, to be so free from any bias in [our] own favor that we can rejoice in our own talents as frankly and gratefully as in our neighbor's talents. (C. S. Lewis, *Screwtape Letters*)

Balance seems to hinge on knowing your abilities, letting other people do the things they are good at, and not feeling guilty you're not doing what others do. (Author Mary Schmal)

TRUTH

 "For we have many members in one body, and not all the members have the same function. In the same way, though we are many, we are one body in Christ, and individually members of one another. We have different gifts, according to the grace God has given us" (Romans 12:4–6).

The gifts mentioned in this passage are to be used to build up and support the family of Christ, "as each part does its work" (Ephesians 4:16 NIV). Would God have designed a body of believers, each with different functions, if each person should *do it all?* To do so risks emotional and physical illness and prideful egotism for members and the church.

With his unique ability to meet people at their level, Paul was successful at being "all things to all people" (1 Corinthians 9:22). But those of us who are not super-apostles will likely burnout[11] trying to please everyone. What a sad, formidable loss for a congregation when someone takes on too much, or others expect him to, resulting in a job resignation.

If you burn yourself out serving and die of
high blood pressure at 50, have you really served

---

[11] Signs of burnout include headaches or muscle tension, trouble with sleeping patterns, feeling cynical, frustration, increased stress, sense of apathy, irritability, feeling unfulfilled, feeling depleted after your workday, and Sunday night blues. If you can identify with many items on this list, please contact your pastor and a professional Christian counselor. If you don't have insurance to cover costs, your congregation may be able to assist. Better to ask for help before the issues become unmanageable.

more than the balanced Christian who served until 80? (Pastor Mike Novotny)

> While there are many things that need to be done, things I'm capable of doing and want to do, I am not always the one to do this. Even if I have a burden for a certain need or project, my interest or concern is not a surefire sign that I need to be in charge… I may be stealing someone else's blessing when I assume I must do it all. (Joanna Weaver, *Having a Mary Heart in a Martha World*)

REFLECTION

How do you know what responsibilities God specifically wants you to do? There is one, certain co-mission each Christian has—to make disciples. With God's blessings, we do outreach corporately in a church body, together in committees or organizations, and individually as we practice "each one teach one" the good news of grace. The mission is not optional.

But what about opportunities for day-to-day tasks of Christian service? Do you say yes to them all? Does the "try and see if I can handle it" method work? When someone sees you in action and says, "You are good at that!" do you take the compliment as confirmation you're doing God's will? If you enjoy a certain task and it comes easily for you to do, it is most likely a gift from God. Let prayer, Christian counsel, and Scripture study direct and bless your serving decisions. And remember, Christian service is not a *have to*, it's a *thank you*.

> If you call out for insight and cry aloud for understanding…then you will understand the fear of the LORD and find the knowledge of God. For the LORD gives wisdom. (Proverbs 2:3–6)

MOTIVATION IDENTIFICATION

Journal and/or discuss your reactions.

1. HAVE YOU IDENTIFIED THINGS IN YOUR LIFE THAT PRE-VENT SMART DECISION-MAKING (ADDICTIONS, RELA-TIONSHIPS, INFLUENCES, ETC.)?

2. IF YOU DON'T CURRENTLY HAVE A MENTOR, WHO CAN YOU ASK TO BE A JETHRO FOR COUNSEL REGARDING OVERWHELMING RESPONSIBILITIES?

3. WHAT PROBLEMS MIGHT YOU FACE WHEN ATTEMPTING TO IMITATE PAUL'S EXAMPLE OF BEING "ALL THINGS TO ALL PEOPLE?"

4. WHAT DO YOU THINK MAKES IT DIFFICULT TO PRIOR-
   ITIZE YOUR CARE OVER THE NEEDS OR REQUESTS OF
   OTHERS?

SELF-CARE INCLUDES SHARING RESPONSIBILITIES WITH OTHERS AND JESUS

The Lord not only knows our need for restoration, he tells us how—by recognizing and relying on him. The Bible is brimming with examples of how he forgives, loves, and cares for his people. God tells us to give all our worries to him, because he is the ultimate provider (1 Peter 5:7, 2 Corinthians 8:8).

"The LORD of Armies is with us. The God of Jacob is a fortress for us. Be still, and know that I am God" (Psalm 34:7, 10).

Like oxen yoked together to plow fields, Jesus walks by our side, supplying strength and support. When we feel the burdensome weight of our sin on our shoulders, he reminds us of the cross that laid on his. We are enabled through Holy Spirit power to be united in kingdom harvest work. When he calls us to serve our family, the church, and others, he shares and lightens our load.

> Take my yoke upon you and learn from me, because I am gentle and humble in heart, and you will find rest for your souls. For my yoke is easy and my burden is light. (Matthew 11:28–30)

PRAYER PROMPT

Thank Jesus for his example of humble service and prayer. Ask him to encourage you in imitating his earthly life: wisely managing work, worship, and rest.

Your prayer space:

PARTICIPATION IN SOCIAL MEDIA, ENTERTAINMENT, GAMING, AND SIMILAR ACTIVITIES PROVIDES STRESS RELIEF

MYTH OR MISUNDERSTANDING

A common habit for relaxation used to be turning on the TV, grabbing a favorite beverage, and getting comfortable in your recliner. Current popular ways to "chill" now involve plugging oneself into technology: music, games, movies, information, communication, or reality escape. The viewing and interacting options for a person with a mere cell phone are unending.

A few minutes on any form of media, and you'll find an improved, surefire way to lose weight effortlessly, build impressive muscles, cook like a pro, remarkably improve life with a simple hack, and "unlock your potential" to do just about anything you wish. You'll also see greed under the guise of increasing consumers' confidence driving a ten-billion-dollar self-help industry. Convenient online purchases make it easy to overspend. Playing electronic games rewards participants with a temporary dopamine rush.

Of course, there are many trustworthy, online companies and responsible providers of harmless fun, and relaxation is not a sin. But there are options to consider. When might sedentary activities (social media, games, shopping, etc.) increase stress? How can we tell which entertainment or social venues refresh our body and soul, and what "easily ensnares us" (Hebrews 12:1)?[12] Are the rating systems for games and movies reliable for God-honoring decisions? Technology is being used to gain and share worthy information around the world, including sharing the gospel. But do a majority of Christians, especially those young in faith or age, realize the desensitizing danger of media that mocks the Savior?

---

[12] Therefore, since we are surrounded by such a great cloud of witnesses, let us get rid of every burden and the sin that so easily ensnares us, and let us run with patient endurance the race that is laid out for us.

MY STRUGGLE

Movies and stage productions stay with me, affecting my thoughts for a long time after I have seen them. Sometimes it's my empathetic personality identifying with a character or situation. My moods are easily influenced by images, music, and plotline. This tendency toward *feeling all the feels* may be emotional immaturity, my extra sensitivity, or both.

Regardless of the reasons, I won't watch a movie or show unless it has been recommended by a trusted source. Perhaps part of this preference is due to seldom experiencing a reality I have a strong desire to escape. Also, I don't care to waste a couple of hours with depressing, dumb, or God-disrespecting *entertainment*.

Unfortunately, my Bible does not have an appendix listing entertainment or recreation activities to avoid. Many relaxation choices fall in the *adiaphora*[13] category. Paul encouraged restraint when judging people whose choices (regarding eating, sacred days, or abstaining from both) reflected their different levels of faith. "The one who eats everything must not look down on him who does not, and the man who does not eat everything must not condemn the man who does, for God has accepted him." The most important reason for this grace-giving attitude is to "not put any stumbling block or obstacle in your brothers' way" so he will continue to follow Christ Jesus (Romans 14: 3, 13 NIV).

Although it's humbling, I need to confess my judgmental tendencies. In my former life as a workaholic, I had a difficult time understanding why everyone was *not* working or volunteering 24/7 (especially for the church)! And for heaven's sake, how could people spend so much money and time on sports and recreation? I could blame my poor attitude on the false application of law and grace. That is certainly part of it. But there was (is?) also my snide thoughts about fun-loving people being spiritually immature. In other words, my sins of arrogance and jealousy were obvious. It often still is! I deeply

---

[13] This term refers to things that are not condemned or condoned in God's Word.

regret giving others a damaging holier-than-thou (or Christians-are-boring) impression.

How often does God need to remind me again to be gentle and respectful to avoid damaging others' faith (1 Peter 3:16, Romans 14:1)?[14] My guilt reaction to such egotistical thoughts is despair, wondering if my sinful motivations ruin God's kingdom work.

> "Who among you, if his son asks him for bread, would give him a stone? Then if you know how to give good gifts to your children, even though you are evil, how much more will your Father in heaven give good gifts to those who ask him!" (Matthew 7:9–11).

I am so thankful my Savior models mercy. He uses pathetic people, even me, to work things out for the good of his kingdom.

> Not many of you were wise from a human point of view… But God chose the foolish things of the world to put to shame those who are wise…to do away with the things that are, so that no one may boast before God. (1 Corinthians 1:26–29)

YOUR STRUGGLE

Social media does help connect and encourage people. Entertainment can provide a needed break from labor, routine, and stress. Playing board and electronic games with family or friends will most often improve those relationships by sharing common fun.

---

[14] "Keeping a clear conscience, so that those who speak maliciously against your good behavior in Christ may be ashamed of their slander"; "Accept the one whose faith is weak, without quarreling over disputable matters."

Have you used activities such as sports to get to know new people? There are churches who host game nights (sports or board type) for bond-building purposes.

> "Entertainment is often good for us. It gives us an evening or a day off from our worries and fears. But when we start living life as entertainment, we lose touch with our souls and become little more than spectators in a lifelong show" (Henri Nouwen).

How do you define (and find) family-friendly entertainment and wholesome recreation? What standards or limits do you use to prevent participation in activities that are not God-pleasing? Have you thought about Romans 12:2 in regard to your relaxation preferences?

> Do not continue to conform to the pattern of this world, but be transformed by the renewal of your mind. (Romans 12:2)

> If God is our pleasure, then pleasure can't be in competition with God. (John Piper, Desiring God Ministries)

TRUTH

Similar to the invention of the moveable type printing press in 1452, the Internet has become a conduit of good and evil. It provides worldwide options for participating in blessings such as online worship services, Bible classes, mission opportunities, and gleaning inspiration from reputable sources. At the same time, this portal opens the door to senseless self-indulgence and addictive behavior for evil.

"Guard what has been entrusted to you, turning away from godless, empty talk and the contradictions of what is falsely called 'knowledge.' By professing it, some have veered away from the faith" (1 Timothy 6:20).

Like me, are you tempted to check your phone first thing in the morning before prayer? Depending on which of these options wins, have you noticed any differences in your day?

> LORD, in the morning you hear my voice. In the morning I lay out my requests in front of you, and I watch for your answer. (Psalm 5:3)

REFLECTION

Is it possible to "make every thought captive so that it is obedient to Christ" (2 Corinthians 10:4–5)? What are some practical ways to pursue this?

Step one, *notice your thought life*. Cognitive behavior theory says when you purposely change your thoughts, it affects your feelings, which, in turn, alters behavior.

Step two, *decipher where your thoughts are coming from* popular opinion, media manipulation, past experiences, misunderstandings, or Christ's truths.

Because our Savior knows what is best for our minds, we need to consistently renew it with his powerful Word. The Holy Spirit empowers us as we learn, memorize, sing, and pray Scripture. Are Bible passages merely in our short-term memory (where worry or distractions easily replace them), or are they a permanent part of our heart? The Word powerfully enables us to "test and approve what is the will of God—what is good, pleasing and perfect" (Romans 12:2b).

> I will not set before my eyes anything that is worthless. (Psalm 101:3 ESV)

But the worries of this life, the deceitfulness of wealth and the desires for other things come in and choke the word, making it unfruitful. (Mark 4:19)

Therefore, after preparing your minds for action by exercising self-control, set your hope fully on the grace that will be brought to you when Jesus Christ is revealed. (1 Peter 1:13)

MOTIVATION IDENTIFICATION

Journal and/or discuss your reactions.

1. HOW DO YOU DECIDE WHICH TECHNOLOGY OR RECREATION IS BENEFICIAL AND WHICH CONTROLS TOO MUCH OF YOUR LIFE?

2. WHICH RECREATIONAL ACTIVITIES HAVE STRENGTHENED YOUR FAITH?

3. DO YOU NOTICE ANY UNPLEASANT EMOTIONAL OR PHYSICAL EFFECTS WHEN YOU UNPLUG FROM TECHNOLOGY OR MEDIA?

4. WHAT'S THE DIFFERENCE BETWEEN PARTAKING IN ENTERTAINMENT OR HOBBIES THAT BENEFIT OUR WELL-BEING AND THOSE ACTIVITIES THAT FILL OUR FREE TIME WITH "FUN" THAT ACTUALLY ADDS MORE STRESS?

GOD-HONORING SELF-CARE AVOIDS UNEDIFYING ENTERTAINMENT AND ACTIVITIES THAT DISRESPECT GOD'S TRUTHS

> I sometimes wonder whether all pleasures are not substitutes for joy. (C. S. Lewis)

> All things are permitted for me—but not all things are beneficial… I will not allow anything to control me. (1 Corinthians 6:12)

Whatever clouds our vision from seeing our spiritual needs harms us. There is a child's hymn that reminds us, "Be careful little eyes what you see…ears, what you hear…feet, where you go." Self-care is not selfish indulgence. It is respectful preservation. It is out of love that our Creator warns people to guard against sin. He knows what nurtures and what destroys us. If we are seeing, hearing, and walking in ways that are contrary to God's will more than in his loving promises, we gradually become oblivious to the damage afflicting our bodies, minds, and souls.

To assist decision-making, resources such as Focus on the Family's Pluggedin.com and Christian Spotlight on Entertainment (Christiananswered.net) reviews movies, TV shows, music, games, and books for family-friendly content. If you are wondering what Jesus would watch, listen to, or play, these websites are excellent guides. Perhaps also you have access to a church library with nurturing G-rated materials.

The Lord gave us free will as a gift. His hope is his children use it to make God-honoring choices.

> Consider carefully, then, how you walk, not as unwise people, but as wise people. Make the most of your time, because the days are evil. (Ephesians 5:15–16)

PRAYER PROMPT

Make a list of entertainment, media, and other recreation you enjoy, noting approximate weekly hours spent on each. Ask God to help you look at this list with his eyes. Confess the sin of participating in any activities if they have led you into temptation. Pray about any changes God prompts you to make. Then remember your complete forgiveness in Christ.

Your prayer space:

AS A PARENT, MY KIDS AND THEIR NEEDS COME BEFORE MINE

MYTH OR MISUNDERSTANDING

Becoming a parent is possibly the most life-changing, challenging, frightening, yet joyous blessing one can receive. When God places a priceless, personalized miracle in your arms, responsibility takes on new meaning. Thinking about and providing for your adult needs while your little one is so dependent seems egotistical, if not immoral. Doesn't a loving parent need to be continuously available for their child?

There's also the nagging guilt of not doing anything well as you are pulled in so many directions: feeding, bathing, changing, rocking, cleaning, learning the latest information of what's best for babies, as well as juggling jobs within and outside of the home. It's easy for Mom and Dad to become overwhelmed by the voices of their consciences, the advising grandparents, their well-meaning friends, and of course, the loud infant cries.

> My big moment of realization that I couldn't do it all—and, believe me, I tried—was when my youngest child (of three) started preschool and I returned to college. The only way I could keep up with all "my responsibility" was by staying up all night once a week to clean, sew, bake, etc. By May, I ended up in the emergency room—an out-of-control bladder infection led to one of my kidneys failing. After a long, miserable recovery that wrecked everyone's summer, I changed totally. I eat right most of the time, work out faithfully, and employ a housekeeper. I was ashamed of delegating the housework for about four minutes, then I recovered. (J. Lonnquist Klebig)

MY STRUGGLE

Loving and raising my three babies was an amazing privilege. It also, however, drained my emotional and physical reserves. Thinking it was a requirement of motherhood, my children's 24/7 needs were continual priorities, while self-nurture was pretty much nonexistent. Especially with my firstborn, it seemed my duty to be hyperaware of the baby's every breath. As I neglected my basic needs for proper amounts of food, sleep, and social connections, it sparked resentment toward my mothering role, then shame. For years I tortured myself with "What kind of a mom resents her kids?" (Answer: an exhausted one.) Thanks to the encouragement and hands-on support from others, I learned to take care of myself and mend the guilt hole.

I often thought of our three little blessings as delayed echoes. If my spouse or I said or did something, it would eventually be repeated. My workaholic tendency to take on too much influenced my children. (Thankfully they have friends and spouses who include them in sabbatical downtime.) Whatever a parent prioritizes, it is providing a model to imitate. And sometimes these tendencies, for better or worse, affect generations.

There's an old parenting quip that says, "Do as I say, not as I do." You can imagine how well that plays out. Chimpanzees are not the only cute little creatures who copy behaviors, good and bad.

> "Start children off on the way they should go, and even when they are old they will not turn from it" (Proverbs 22:6 NIV).

Several years ago I purchased an antique tin watering can at a garage sale. I enjoyed using it around my deck until rust broke through the bottom. Instead of sadly throwing it away, I painted and repurposed it as part of a garden display. When my children matured and left home, I felt as useless as a rusty, leaky container. So much of my life had revolved around their abundant needs and busy schedules. I didn't expect an empty nest to feel like grief or to last so long.

Perhaps my parenting habits of dismissing my own self-care added increased difficulty in repurposing myself. [15]

YOUR STRUGGLE

Admittedly there are days, months, or sometimes years, when self-care is extra difficult. The sleepless nights with a crying newborn is one such season. During this kind of stress, it's especially vital for parents to prioritize their rest and be hyperaware of time robbing, unimportant distractions. One example is taking a "quick peek" at social media. Suddenly, it seems you are in an Internet time warp where hours magically disappear. Reboot and restart your thoughts by unplugging your brain from electronics.

Who has God made you responsible for in your current stage of life? If you are a parent, are you continuing the rest-versus-work pattern you learned in your family of origin? Most likely, your parents did the best job they could from the information they had. But if your mom often seemed exhausted and overwhelmed in her mothering role, please find encouraging counsel and reliable support so you don't repeat the pattern. Feel free to ask others about best parenting practices for your current situation and what might assist. Stress-induced, no-relief parenting can lead to dangerous zombie-like functioning.

Your circumstances are always changing and your self-care needs change with them. We need to understand which area of self-care needs our attention most, what is getting in our way, and which resources we have in front of us to help. (Carly Laabs)

---

[15] I am thankful for the help gleaned from the book *Barbara and Susan's Guide to the Empty Nest* (Bethany House).

TRUTH

The Wagners are a close-knit family in my community. Every birthday and holiday is an opportunity to get the entire fifteen-member clan together and celebrate. The love and connectedness seem admirable except for one thing: no one person can make a decision until all members are consulted.

Enmeshment is a term used to describe a relationship where one is so over-involved in the other's affairs it handicaps autonomous development. Individuals can protect themselves from this emotional control by establishing personal boundaries. Boundaries let others know, "I understand you feel that way, but I see things differently" and "I am doing what I need to do to take care of myself." Its purpose is to prevent enmeshment, and disconnect from the behavior of another, especially necessary in abusive situations. Boundaries clarify responsibilities. Because we can't control the opinions and actions of others, boundaries are necessary for mental health. To reinforce these helpful limits, we may need to avoid or physically remove ourselves from boundary-usurping (i.e., controlling) people and situations. These parameters also protect us from emotional overload, which in turn prevents thoughtless reactions, blame, and "what about me?" arguments.

We show respect to our and the other person's ability to self-govern by establishing responsibility boundaries. In a marriage, these agreements give each partner the freedom to love without coercion, while respecting differences. Instead of relying on others to complete our identity (enmeshment), healthy boundaries will strengthen dependency on our trustworthy God. We look to him for help with decisions, directions, and behavior, instead of other people.

> "Each person has the right to maintain a separate self that is accountable to God and independent of the expectations, the approval or influence of others" (Kock & Haugk, *Speaking the Truth in Love—How to Be an Assertive Christian*).

Children learn about boundaries when a parent sets limits on how much personal space and time the kids can occupy. Are their toys permitted in every room? Do Mom and Dad enjoy activities without the rest of the family? Consistency in rules, rewards, and results of misbehavior are boundaries that provide security in a loving home.

> "Discipline your son, and he will give you rest. He will give delight to your soul" (Proverbs 29:17).

Parents who do not take care of themselves are like the gardener who neglects to build a fence (boundary) around her vegetable plants. No matter how much effort put into weeding and watering, the gardener gleans nothing, while neighborhood rabbits grow fat.

Of course, it is difficult to put these emotional margins between you and your children because *they are only little once* and they are so needy (and cute)! Similar to the need for at least six hours of sleep, Mommy and Daddy wellness also requires pauses in parenting tasks. Yes, there are days and nights and weeks when parenting time off is not practical or possible. But that's when you ask, seek, and find assistance. Does your congregation offer playgroups or other respite opportunities? Might you suggest starting one? What community groups and friends are available?

REFLECTION

Are you waiting for a magical, star-aligning time to add self-care to your priorities? Do you promise to do it when the kids are older, your job changes, the church finds another volunteer, your spouse helps more, or when you are retired? Gardens do not provide a harvest of blessings without boundaries, nourishment, and proper attention. Neither do parents.

Note the benefits for others, as well as for yourself, as you slowly transition from unhealthy habits to self-respecting boundaries. You may need to have tangible reinforcements until your behavior feels natural. For example, when I held up my finger and said, "Let me finish this thought," to a friend who habitually interrupted, I pictured myself getting a pat on the back. When I communicated what hostess tasks I'd be happy to do and which ones someone else would need to handle, it resulted in a more relaxed, enjoyable get-together.

As you align new priorities, expect adjustments for yourself and the others affected by them. In the short term, reward yourself for the positive adaptations. In the long run, your improved welfare will be worthy of a celebration!

> It is not so much about balance as it is about priorities. When I realized I had choices about how to respond, take action or step back until I knew more what to do, things changed. I began making more life adjustments with more confidence. (Robin Fry)

> We need to give ourselves permission to embrace both godly humility and godly pride… godly generosity and godly asset accumulation… care for others and self-care…carrying each other's burdens and setting boundaries. (Pastor Mark Jeske)

MOTIVATION IDENTIFICATION

Journal and/or discuss your reactions.

1. WHERE SHOULD LINES BE DRAWN BETWEEN VIGILANT PARENTAL CONCERN AND FRETFUL WORRY OVER CHILDREN?

2. HOW HAS YOUR EXPERIENCE WITH LOVING YOUR CHILDREN (OR OTHERS') EXPANDED YOUR APPRECIATION OF "GOD IS LOVE?"

3. LIST WAYS YOUR FAMILY HAS SABOTAGED YOUR SELF-CARE EFFORTS. WHAT MIGHT BE SOME WAYS TO AVOID OR DIFFUSE SIMILAR SITUATIONS?

4. WHAT PERSONAL BOUNDARIES HAVE YOU ENACTED IN YOUR HOME OR WORKPLACE?

SUMMARY: GOD-HONORING SELF-CARE INCLUDES PERSONAL BOUNDARIES AND PARENTING SUPPORT

When going anywhere with a little one, think of all the essential items included in their diaper bag. Loving parents plan ahead for their child's care. Is predicting your own needs any less important? Have you, like me, remembered to take food along for the kids but would forget to eat until feeling faint? Are you able to joyfully encourage and provide for others, while feeling hungry and drained?

There will be many days when it is difficult to plan how and when to be your own concerned caregiver. But it is a stewardship principle for your body and sanity. Remember, the Lord is eager to hear and answer your prayers for wisdom regarding help in this.

> As a father has compassion on his children,
> so the LORD has compassion on those who fear
> him. (Psalm 103:13)

> Whatever you ask for in prayer, as you believe, you will receive. (Matthew 21:22)

PRAYER PROMPT

Praise God for the fresh joys and wonder children (our own or others) bring into our lives. Ask your Heavenly Father to bless and encourage all the parents you know. Name those who may be especially struggling.

Your prayer space:

SELF-CARE IS JUST NOT FEASIBLE IN SOME VOCATIONS

MYTH OR MISUNDERSTANDING

There are employees, especially in church or charity work, who feel they are ignoring their God-given calling when they take breaks from responsibilities. Some people do not take a personal day off, much less a vacation, even when it's recommended. They feel working excessively is expected for their job position.

Other individuals assertively pursue personal health activities and have relaxing hobbies. They believe enjoying nonwork-related activities is rejuvenating, enabling more effective and joyful service. They understand the renewing benefits of this balance.

Might there be some vocations where allowance for self-care is not practical or possible?

Athletes don't attempt to compete without training or using proper protective equipment. Buildings need to be constructed using specific safety regulations. Are there any engines or machines that run without some kind of fuel and upkeep? Why then would the complex systems of our mind and body be expected to function unaided?

Before the Reformation, the monk Martin Luther used self-mortification in attempts to become worthy of God. Serving the church while denying self is still regarded as a high calling by many, especially those in Roman Catholic religious orders.

Do Christian vocations have more value than other jobs?

> Every occupation has its own honor before God. Ordinary work is a divine vocation or calling. In our daily work no matter how important or mundane we serve God by serving the neighbor. (Martin Luther)

> It's really not the church that runs our lives, it's our personal gifts and how we use them to serve the Lord no matter where we are. (Susan Ann Lueneburg)

Pastors, teachers, staff ministers, and others in church work are often expected to be performing duties or to be on call continuously. Is it possible for those in ministry to serve faithfully and yet be proactive for their health? If you are in church work, be bold and ask for consistent, fair time off! You will be setting a healthy example for others to imitate.

Similar to church- and charity-related jobs, healthcare providers of their loved ones can view their duties as an exhausting burden or as an opportune blessing. Compassionate helpers may experience both these reactions, even at the same time! Are you a caregiver for a family member or friend? It is critical to have respite assistance for these situations. There are far too many people who get seriously ill while attempting to do and be everything for their ailing loved ones.

Compassion fatigue is a common malady among those in caring professions. It causes self-doubt, distress, and even apathy. How might congregations encourage their leaders to avoid this?

> I have come to the conclusion that having a balance in life is nearly impossible to achieve. The goal needs to be building a healthy rhythm. There will be times that ministry dominates, times that the family dominates, and time for self. We need to put on our own oxygen mask first and make sure we are solidly grounded in God and His word, to be spiritually, emotionally and physically resilient. (Greg Schmill)

> I think trying to maintain a balance leaves us feeling guilty. (Linda Buxa)

Individuals vary regarding what is necessary for their self-preservation. For instance, some people have high energy levels and low sleep requirements. But for everyone, there are occasions when saying *no* to "going above and beyond" is the optimal, healthiest response.

Effective self-care also requires discernment on what work to take on and what to delegate or even leave undone. Being caught up with work life has often contributed to leaders falsely believing that they do not have enough time for self-care because getting work done for God is more important. Unfortunately, though it may sound honorable, it is far from true. (Dr. Jonathan Lotson, *Effective Leadership*, Christian Faith Publishing)

For many educators, the 2020 COVID-19 pandemic forced a quick transition to virtual learning. A grade-school music teacher told me how difficult it was to quickly adjust and teach individual instrument lessons online. The stress weakened her immune system, resulting in a painful viral infection.

When I was a young Christian grade school teacher I would give up sleep to get more done (practice organ, correct papers, contact parents, etc.) but then I had less patience and love for my students. (Greg Schmill)

My parents were both servant leaders, doing their work with great joy. I loved going with my dad when he was asked to preach somewhere. When I had a question, problem, or situation, my dad dropped what he was doing to talk with me. He worked out in his huge garden to care for his body. After a busy day typing, cooking, cleaning, Mom would read. That was her self-care. Both of my parents exercised. Mom did through her 101 years!

A huge factor in balancing work with fun or relaxation was going to our cottage on a lake in Wisconsin. How I loved that place which my father and his father built together in 1939 as (farmer Grandpa Lawrenz said) "a necessity get-away for a busy minister. (Mary Schmal)

MY STRUGGLE

Have you experienced employment that required long hours, answering messages from home, or other work responsibilities during your *free time*? For ten years I worked as a director of volunteers for a hospice program. It was so rewarding at first; the extra demands and donations for the sake of the program weren't cumbersome. My prayer was that my words and actions would reflect Christ's light, especially to unbelieving coworkers. In many instances, my attempts at humility were met with suspicion. Thinking I was demonstrating compassion and patience, I didn't defend myself against false accusations and miscommunication. Instead of learning from our work team's mistakes, I was expected to cover them over. When a volunteer rightly pointed out an error made by my boss, I was told to *fire* the volunteer. My refusal to do so was regarded as being rudely rebellious. In discussing this quandary with our hospice chaplain, his advice was to decide what I valued more—my feelings or my job.

This same employer required unpaid attendance at flashy concert-like cheering events to convince employees to surpass exceedingly high expectations. Eventually, the repeated mantras of "you aren't doing enough…not loyal enough" drove me to frustrated tears and years of professional counseling. The Lord rescued me when, along with many others, I was terminated.

I had not realized how toxic my job situation had been until I was out of that oppressive atmosphere. While talking to my next-door neighbor (who knew my situation), I commented on all the beautiful new birds in our yards. "Sue," she said, "those birds have always been here. You were so stressed you never noticed them before."

When Jesus redirects us, our eyes see more of the good.

Consider how the wild flowers grow. They
do not labor or spin. But I tell you, not even
Solomon in all his glory was dressed like one of
these. (Luke 12:27)

🏃 YOUR STRUGGLE

Do you feel selfish turning someone down, especially if it has to do with a deserving, benevolent cause?

Like me, do you work or volunteer more hours and put in much more effort because of an approval addiction? There is also the "what-will-others-think-if-I-don't" motivation or the prideful "If I don't do it, it won't get done or get done correctly."

There are occasions when investing in your well-being is extra important. Think of some tense times in your life: final exams as a college student, a creative or athletic performance, planning an important event, moving, preparing for an extended vacation, or similar stress. We all know someone who became ill or depressed when their scale was tipped too far in the neglect-my-own-needs position.

To make long-range financial decisions, an investor trusts his company to have experts who carefully study forecasts and risks. Do you have a plan for your physical risk management? Does your goal setting involve assessing spiritual as well as emotional gains and debts? Self-discipline and prayed-for discernment will add valuable deposits to your health bank.

What good will it be for a man if he gains
the whole world, yet forfeits his soul? Or what can
a man give in exchange for his soul? (Matthew
16:26)

TRUTH

Long work hours and lack of rest in any profession contribute to stress-related conditions and diseases, strained (or terminated) relationships, and early retirement. Professionals and volunteers in people-helping charities are at high risk. Do you check in on your pastor(s), leaders, teachers, and overachievers, encouraging them to enjoy a hobby and schedule some fun? Pausing from responsibilities is vital to relieve strain and restore energy.

A restless work style produces a restless person; we do not rest because our work is done; we rest because God commanded it and created us to have a need for it. (Author Gordon MacDonald)

At age sixty-two the Lord told me, "You're done."

I thought I could do it all, being a principal, doing 160 teacher observations a year and many hours every night of paperwork. I thought doing things to the very best of my ability meant taking no breaks, not getting a proper amount of sleep, working on Sundays, etc. My job consumed me. In November I had a mini-stroke, my blood pressure was 220. The doctor said I was lucky.

I went back to my long rushed schedule too soon. Then in March my appendix blew up. I couldn't get off the floor. I was in so much pain. The doctor said I was very lucky, "This could have killed you." I lost twenty pounds and set a boundary that I would go to bed at 10:00 p.m. I did my job, but just the basics, and thought, "Why have I been killing myself? Even God rested on the seventh day."

My self-care now includes walking four miles a day or I swim. I feel younger now than I did ten years ago. We need to care enough about others, especially those in church work, to tell them to *rest*. (Keith Wakeman)

I felt there were higher expectations and more responsibilities placed on me because of my firstborn status. That carried over into my many years of teaching for the church as I attempted to meet everyone's expectations. Also, I was surrounded by those who were so busy serving their congregation and school, there was little time or attention for family. We need to tell called workers it is okay, actually healthy, to say no. (Arlyss Troge)

When Jesus taught his followers, "Be perfect, as your heavenly Father is perfect" (Matthew 5:48), was he encouraging them to pursue righteousness through works? Thinking you are heaven-bound only if you are obviously working for God's kingdom is works righteousness sin. Listen to the use of the words *always*, *never*, and *should*. "You *should* be accomplishing something for God every day." "Her former pastor *always* visited each shut-in once a week, so I *should* also." "My mom was admired because she *never* took a vacation." These absolutes are most often connected to law-based or validation-seeking motives. The cure is to remember who approves and controls the results of our labor. In grateful response to God's love, Christians seek his direction as we begin and finish what "God prepared in advance for us to do" (Ephesians 2:10 NIV). The devil, on the other hand, loves to promote prideful workaholism.[16]

---

[16] "Workaholism is the compulsion or uncontrollable need to work incessantly" (Oates 1971).

When we get messed up on sinful motivations, like control and approval seeking, it is generally because we are falling for Satan's lies. (Greg Schmill)

God's approval isn't based on what a person does. Rather, he accepts what a person does because he already approves of the person. The person hasn't earned God's approval through the good that he or she does. (Martin Luther, *Faith Alone: A Daily Devotional*)

Legalism says we have to *do this and accomplish that*. The full gospel gently shows we are being made holy (sanctified), but *we are already perfect through him*.

"In fact, the law is only a shadow of the good things to come, not the actual realization of those things. By only one sacrifice he has made perfect forever those who are being sanctified" (Hebrews 10:14).

REFLECTION

How might you include time for your needs amid stringent job requirements or long-term volunteer opportunities? Be confident in the necessity of self-care and practice polite assertiveness. Can you say "Yes, but—" to requests and add stipulations? "Sure, I can be a greeter at church one Sunday a month, but who can I call on short notice if something comes up?" "Yes, I would take on part of that job but can only give two hours a day." "I have prayed about it, and I need to say no. But thanks for thinking of me."

How might you commit to taking some self-compassion action? Try fitting your prayed-about priorities under broad categories like *faith, family, health*. Then narrow these down into goal statements. What reminders might motivate you? Give yourself grace and allow for flexibility. Remember it takes twenty-one days of consistency before an activity becomes a habit. Hang in there, and in three months you'll say hello to your new normal.

> Let people do the things God gave them gifts to do, and not feel guilty you are not doing those same things. It takes very little for an aggrieved person in our lives to shame us and make us feel as if we've been neglecting him or her: we also beat ourselves up pretty good. My counsel is to confess your sins to Jesus, bask in his unconditional forgiveness, pour a glass of wine, sit in your favorite chair, let everything go, and then sleep well. (Pastor Mark Jeske)

MOTIVATION IDENTIFICATION

Journal and/or discuss your reactions.

1. IF WE LOSE ABILITIES AS WE AGE OR BECOME DEPEN-
    DENT ON OTHERS FOR OUR ACTIVITIES OF DAILY LIVING,
    WHAT REGRETS MIGHT WE HAVE?

2. HAVE YOU EXPERIENCED BEING UNAWARE OF A TOXIC SITUATION UNTIL YOU WERE OUT OF IT? WHAT WARN-ING SIGNS DID THAT EXPERIENCE HELP YOU TO LOOK OUT FOR?

3. DO YOU THINK OF YOURSELF AS PERFECT? (SEE HEBREWS 10:14.)

4. WHEN MIGHT A JOB OR CAREER BECOME IDOLATRY OR SIN AGAINST THE THIRD COMMANDMENT?

SUMMARY: SAYING NO TO WORK OVERLOAD IS NOT SELFISH

Are you currently employed in a way that weakens or threatens your well-being? Does it seem your employer is pushing you toward burnout? Find out if your loved ones are feeling ignored due to the demands of your job. Prayerfully and assertively take steps to change any abusive situation. Be emboldened to ask God for discernment and seek counsel from trusted medical and spiritual care sources. If you need to temporarily endure suffering, ask the Holy Spirit to grant you a Christlike attitude, reflecting his light to others.

PRAYER PROMPT

Verbalize gratefulness to Christ and to all you know who wholeheartedly work to expand his kingdom. Confidently bring all the questions and concerns you have about self-care to his throne. Ponder and take heart that Christ has forgiven you. Your prayer space:

WE ARE SO SECURE IN JESUS, WE DON'T NEED TO CARE FOR OUR SELF

MYTH OR MISUNDERSTANDING

This chapter's title is more of a misunderstood half-truth than a myth. All people are "God's own possession" (1 Peter 2:9), thanks to his Son's obedient, law-fulfilling life, atoning debt-paying death, and his victorious resurrection. Since (as C. S. Lewis explains) God is a gentleman; he does not force this grace unto those who "harden their hearts" (Psalm 95:7) and reject it. Through faith, all believers enjoy an eternal, perfect, "Sabbath rest... For the one who enters God's rest also rests from his own work" (Hebrews 4:9–10). No amount of effort on our part inches us any closer to earning this gospel gift.

Matthew writes about a time when Jesus, grieving the violent death of his cousin John, "withdrew...in a boat to a deserted place to be alone" (14:13). God-man as he was, he became distraught and tired. Did he ignore his need for rest?

> After he had dismissed the crowds, he went up onto the mountain by himself to pray. When evening came, he was there alone. (Matthew 14:13–14, 23)

> Jesus had compassion on the hungry crowds that followed him, but didn't feel guilty about getting away from them. (Pastor Mike Novotny)

While we tend to run from project to project, our Lord's *modus operandi* was walking. If never-sinning Jesus intentionally took time away from his mission, for prayer and restoration, how can we claim we don't need the same?

> Self-care is finding our rest in tune with our Savior. (Lisa Miller)

> One of the things my strength training instructor emphasized was the importance of let-

ting my muscles rest between sets… Our muscles need that short one to two minute time to recover and this rest time actually helps build stronger muscles and prevent damage. Our lives are the same way. We cannot keep working without a rest. God has designed us—physically, spiritually, and emotionally—for a healthy rhythm of work and rest. Resting may often seem like a frivolous pursuit, but in truth it's the best thing we can do to stay strong—for ourselves and for those around us. ("Developing the Habit of Rest," EdieMelson.com)

MY STRUGGLE

The woman described in Proverbs 31 is praised for her respectful fear of the Lord and her many accomplishments. Harmonious with Jesus's exhortation not to "worry about tomorrow" (Matthew 6:34), this prepared wife and mom calmly "laughs at the days to come." Her confident trust is a trait I most often lack. Sinfully, I tend to dwell on the "what-ifs" instead of taking comfort in God's past provisions and sovereign plan.

Additionally, my anxiety increases when I forget to pray or when I rush through a Bible reading. Yet this behavior is repeated so often! Praise God for his patience. He keeps forgiving and urging me to "approach the throne of grace with *confidence*, so that we may receive mercy and find grace to help us in our time of [spiritual] need" (Hebrews 4:16).

I also tend to forget how my behavior and emotions interact. Getting sufficient sleep, eating more vegetables than cookies, spending meaningful time with loved ones, and setting goals will powerfully affect one's mental health. People are a chemical soup of serotonin (effecting sleep and depression), dopamine (emotion and cognition), glutamate (memory and learning), norepinephrine (stress response), and many other complicated body and brain connectors.

Scientists have found new neural pathways are created in our brains when we complete a task, meditate, play with a puppy, give compliments, laugh, tend flowers, and show appreciation.

YOUR STRUGGLE

Do you treat yourself as kindly as you do your friends? Would you say those same harsh words to anyone else? Or to your dog? Positive mental health care includes positive self-talk. Self-condemnation is not humility.

What is the bottom-line source of our own negative voices?

"Another mistake, you better give up!"

"You are so worthless, don't even try. Why would God use you for anything?"

"How stupid can you be?"

Those are quips from the father of lies himself. He wants you to grovel in despair so you stop being a witness of God's gifts in and to you. Don't give the devil a foothold! Instead, surround yourself with believers and Bible promises to remind you how precious you are. You are God's redeemed—a treasured lamb for whom he will leave the other ninety-nine to rescue. Sins removed with love, adopted through grace—that is the truth of who you are!

Be strong in the Lord and in his mighty power. Put on the full armor of God, so that you can stand against the schemes of the devil. (Ephesians 6:10–11)

See what great love the Father has lavished on us, that we should be called children of God! (1 John 3:1)

TRUTH

Jesus observed the Sabbath. The Old Testament Sabbath ordinances reflected God's rest from work on the seventh day of creation (Genesis 2:1–3) and celebrating freedom from Egyptian oppression (Deuteronomy 5:6–12). Although the manna-collecting Israelites were slow to catch on, Moses directed, "Look, the LORD has given you the Sabbath. Therefore on the sixth day he will give you two days' worth of bread. So the people rested on the seventh day" (Exodus 16:29–30).

God didn't maximize productivity, work or service. Built into the Old Testament calendar was rest and lots of it. (Pastor Mike Novotny)

One of the ways you can move forward toward self-care is by observing a weekly Sabbath—a 24-hour block of time in which you rest and contemplate God. (Dr. Jonathan Lotson, *Effective Leadership*, Christian Faith Publishing)

Paul explained how keeping the Sabbath (ceasing labor to worship and restore our relationship with God) is no longer mandatory (Colossians 2:16).[17] But its value has multiplied exponentially. We now have shalom (Hebrew for peace, harmony, completeness, wellness, and calmness) in the eternal rest Christ won for us.

Resting is a work of faith. (Pastor Daron Lindemann)

If you keep the Sabbath, you start to see creation not as somewhere to get away from your

---

[17] "Therefore, do not let anyone judge you in regard to food or drink, or in regard to a festival or a New Moon or a Sabbath day."

ordinary life, but a place to frame attentiveness to your life. (Author Eugene H. Peterson)

The law of God was clear for Israel: There was to be no work or play on the Sabbath. If we aren't bound by those restrictions, as Jesus made clear, then does the Sabbath matter at all? The answer is yes, because the essence of the Sabbath day—and, hand in hand with it, the essence of the Third Commandment—was rest and renewal primarily for the soul. (Pastor Jared Natsis)

REFLECTION

The shepherd-turned-king David writes how his "soul rests quietly in God alone" (Psalm 62:1) even when facing numerous earthly enemies.

"In complete peace I will lie down, and I will sleep, for you alone, O Lord, make me dwell in safety" (Psalm 4:8).

How might you glean this confidence of peaceful rest?

Think of Jesus's examples of defeating Satan's distortions of Scripture (by using Scripture), distancing himself from miracle-seeking crowds, and his frequent communication with the Father. As a man, Jesus had to discipline himself to learn the Word, know his body's need for rest, and develop a dependence on prayer. Do you imitate these disciplines on a regular basis?

"God's Word is perfect in every way; how it revives our souls! His laws lead us to truth, and his ways change the simple into wise" (Psalm 19:7 The Passion Translation).

Every day on social media, my friend Darci optimistically lists three more things she is grateful for, even while enduring unpleasant cancer treatments. She encourages her many friends by listing the blessings God helps her to see. How might you express thanks for a new blessing every day? Could you keep this up for one month? One year?

Are you connected to a nurturing faith community that strengthens your battle against spiritual atrophy? Do you have friends that model self-discipline? Have you asked a sister or brother in Christ to pray about and urge you to recharge your spirit? Mature spiritual leaders know the importance of relationships with trusted mentors. Find an accountability partner who is a good listener and encourager. Perhaps you can mentor each other by sharing mutual goals, prayers, and blessings.

> Therefore, encourage one another and build each other up, just as you are also doing. (1 Thessalonians 5:11)

> Commit what you do to the LORD, and your plans will be established. (Proverbs 16:3)

MOTIVATION IDENTIFICATION

Journal and/or discuss your reactions.

1. DOES RESPECTING YOUR NEEDS DISRESPECT JESUS'S ADMONITION NOT TO WORRY ABOUT WHAT WE EAT, DRINK, OR WEAR?

2. HOW IS THE SABBATH PRINCIPLE APPLIED IN YOUR LIFE?

3. WHO HAS ENCOURAGED YOUR FAITH? HAVE YOU THANKED THEM RECENTLY?

4. IS PRAYER A CONSISTENT PART OF YOUR DAY?

GOD-GLORIFYING SELF-CARE INCLUDES SELF-RESPECT AND SABBATH REST

We don't expect seeds to grow without soil, water, or sun. Our bodies also have requirements. Ignoring them makes us weak, sometimes to the point of not recognizing the problem. Like a sleep-deprived college student (existing on pizza and caffeine), our thinking is clouded. Correspondingly, ignoring faith growth opportunities will result in stagnant, fruitless lives.

> "How blessed is the man who does not walk in the advice of the wicked… But his delight is in the teaching of the LORD, and on his teaching he meditates day and night. He is like a tree planted beside streams of water, which yields its fruit in season, and its leaves do not wither" (Psalm 1:1–3).

Wise mental health counselors and doctors know their own self-care is essential. Without it, they are more likely to make poor decisions, with the possibility of causing harm to themselves and their patients.

We have the ultimate reason to be good stewards of our bodies and lives; in humble gratitude that Almighty God chooses us to glorify him.

> Offer the members of your body to God as tools of righteousness. (Romans 6:13)

> There is within you a lamb and a lion. Spiritual maturity is the ability to let lamb and lion lie down together. When you heed only your lion, you will find yourself overextended and exhausted. (Author Henri Nouwen)

PRAYER PROMPT

Confess your sin of worry. Name your concerns and ask in Jesus's name to replace them with reminders of his promises. Confess the ways you disrespect yourself. Thank your Savior for hearing and answering your prayers.
Your prayer space:

I'M TOO BUSY
FOR SELF-CARE

MYTH OR MISUNDERSTANDING

Ode to the Rushed Life

I have no time for friendships, my job demands long days,
There's homework with the kids, then putting toys away.
No personal time for reading, can't squeeze in Bible time,
There's shopping, cleaning, chauffeuring—all are tasks of mine.
Meal preparation, eating—all have to be done real quick,
Too busy to help a neighbor, or church member who is sick.
I promise I'll slow down soon, to worship, pray, and rest,
But until I'm lying sick in bed, rushing's what I do best.

Is it honestly possible to not have room in your schedule for self-nurture? Are you convinced you can survive (at least temporarily) while neglecting your body and soul? How are your responsibilities and thinking affected when tired or ill?

The modern inventions of the dishwasher, computers, and robot vacuum cleaners were supposed to add leisure time to our lives. So why does the friendly greeting "How are you?" most often get an eye-rolling "Busy!" response? Has a hectic agenda without breathing room become a status symbol in our culture?

"God says slow down!" (Chuck Swindoll,
Living on the Ragged Edge).

In the book *Crazy Busy*, Pastor Kevin DeYoung warns of three dangers for overscheduled Christians: it can ruin joy, rob hearts, and cover up the rot in our souls. Does the Lord want his children to be striving constantly without enjoying pleasantries like humor, music, food, and fun? In the midst of self-made hectic days and nights, when are we able to pause and focus on blessings?

It is useless for you to get up early and to
work late, worrying about bread to eat, because

God grants sleep to the one he loves. (Psalm 127:2)

> For what does a man gain through all his hard work, through all the turmoil in his heart, as he works so hard under the sun? Pain fills all his days. His occupation is frustration. Even at night his heart does not rest. This too is vapor. (Ecclesiastes 2:23)

King Solomon, to whom God gave the gift of wisdom, was most likely the author of these poetic lines: "There is an appropriate time for every activity under heaven…a time to weep and a time to laugh, a time to mourn and a time to dance… Also, when anyone eats, drinks, and experiences the good things that his hard work leads to—this is God's gift" (Ecclesiastes 3:1–4, 13). Does this sound like a recipe for hurried, harried days and nights?

MY STRUGGLE

In my not-so-distant past, I thought my busyness was evidence of my purpose and worth. And, wow, does checking my phone, Facebook, and e-mails keep me busy! Those rings and pings make any recipient feel important. Experts say social media is designed that way on purpose—to give us little dopamine highs when we receive messages and emojis. When I neglect to nurture myself, I look for ways of getting it from others. Unfortunately, my quick check for virtual encouragement posts can turn into a two-hour marathon. That bad habit of unnecessary, artificial busyness contributes to spiritual dehydration.

> "The best thing about going to Yellowstone or Glacier National Park is that all cellphone service doesn't work and no one can get a hold of you" (Pastor Dean Zemple).

What else causes me to hurry? Taking a look at my typical routines reveals sleeping two hours longer than my body needs, wasting time watching silly YouTube videos, and not preplanning meals which result in extra grocery runs. Where did I put that list of resolutions I made for this year? And goals for this month?

The tyranny of hurry usurps the preventative care which doctors and therapists recommend. It has become common for health insurance companies to pay for wellness physical exams. Some will cover the cost of exercise classes and activity trackers. Less money is spent, and there's less suffering for the patient if disease prevention or early detection is done. *Self-care is a priority because it is preventative care.*

YOUR STRUGGLE

> Busyness and noise are anesthetics to dull our pain. (Pastor Tom Pankow)

Was there ever a time you kept yourself busy in order to cope with an unpleasant situation?

When the mother of five young girls died, my friend was hired as a caregiver. Brenda not only did all the housework, cooking, and child care; she comforted and loved the grieving daughters as if they were her own. "Staying active in church, joining the choir, ladies' group, and Bible class were the things that kept me sane," Brenda said about those demanding days. "My sense of humor did help, but also I never dwelled on the difficult things I was going through. I was much too busy."

If you live with a crammed full schedule, have you reflected on a reason? When you are busy, do you feel guilty, anxious, or unable to concentrate when attempting to pause? Our fast-paced, information-overload culture tempts us to forget the benefits of quiet introspection. Trying to live in the peace of Jesus while busyness rules your schedule is akin to singing a lullaby in a roomful of loud, crying babies. What noises redirect your focus from God's calming voice?

There will always be one more task to finish, one more e-mail to answer, one or more things on our *urgent* list that didn't get done. This will be true until we lay still in our coffins. Then, what will have mattered most?

> It was a great moment in my adult life when I realized that life was meant to be enjoyed rather than simply endured. (Chuck Swindoll, *Living on the Ragged Edge*)

TRUTH

If we believe the Lord has graciously given us relationships, responsibilities, and purpose, can't we assume he will give us adequate minutes to accomplish what he wills us to do?

His prescription for our uncomfortable, pulled-in-different-directions hurriedness is to "Be still and know that I am God" (Psalm 46:10). He yearns to lead us away from distractions, to the safe, quiet waters of contentment. Being still includes removing self-made urgencies and relinquishing worldly concerns. This frees us to enjoy his calming, renewing presence. The provider of all seasons directs us to "Consider carefully, then, how you walk, not as unwise people, but as wise people. Make the most of your time...understand[ing] what the will of the Lord is" (Ephesians 5:16–17). This antithesis of anxiety promises true peace.

REFLECTION

Do you consider yourself a mindful person—able to be attentive to your surroundings? Unlike the Middle Eastern meditation practice of attempting to erase all thoughts, mindfulness is using your senses to notice small, positive things. It's a way of bringing things from your subconscious to your conscious state.

Christians want to be purposely aware of heavenly things (Colossians 3:2). Mindfulness includes immersing oneself in the present, using nonjudgmental observation skills. Brain research says a mindful approach optimizes mental health, minimizes chronic pain and insomnia, and improves the immune system. All of this also impacts emotional behavior, which increases empathy, compassion, and improves decision-making ability.

Here is an activity to promote your self-awareness.

On a computer or piece of paper, draw intersecting lines to make twenty-four squares. Using each square to represent one hour, write (or color, using a code) how you usually spend those hours. For an honest look at your typical schedule, do this for at least two weeks.

Does the completed visual show you anything surprising? Note the nonessential activities. Which of these could you give up? Are the mini-tasks you do significant or urgent? Could anything be altered to reflect better priorities? After making these observations, ask the Lord to give you the wisdom to pause, pray, and plan according to his will.

> If any one of you lacks wisdom, let him ask God, who gives it to all without reservation and without finding fault, and it will be given to him. (James 1:5)

> Teach us to number our days that we may gain a heart of wisdom. (Psalm 90:12 NIV)

MOTIVATION IDENTIFICATION

Journal and/or discuss your reactions.

1. WHY MIGHT SATAN ENJOY OBSERVING BUSYNESS AMONG CHRISTIANS?

2. IN ENGLAND, "GOING ON HOLIDAY" (FROM "HOLY DAY" IN OLD ENGLISH) MEANS TAKING A VACATION. HOW DO YOU DECIDE WHEN AND HOW LONG TO TAKE A VACATION?

3. HOW DOES YOUR IDENTITY IN CHRIST INFLUENCE YOUR SCHEDULE?

4. HOW MIGHT MINDFULNESS AFFECT YOUR OUTLOOK? WHAT HURDLES DO YOU FORESEE?

GOD-DIRECTED SELF-CARE AVOIDS UNWISE BUSYNESS

When we are enslaved to misguided priorities, we are unable to provide for our health, pray unhurriedly, nor mindfully meditate on God's powerful Word. Hectic schedules with long to-do lists rob our energy to live out his purposes. Thankfully, we can ask the Lord to reveal the false motives for our rushed daily grind. With his guidance, we can know and honor our true needs and responsibilities with humble, grateful hearts.

> And everything you do, whether in word or deed, do it all in the name of the Lord Jesus, giving thanks to God the Father through him. (Colossians 3:17)

> The proud man and the covetous man never have rest, but the meek man and the poor in spirit live in great abundance of rest and peace. (Thomas Kempis)

> Blessed are those who hunger and thirst for righteousness, because they will be filled. (Matthew 5:6)

PRAYER PROMPT

As you review this book's information, what questions or concerns remain unanswered? Feel free to ask your loving Savior. What might you need to confess? Ask spiritual leaders and friends to pray for you and with you. Thank the Almighty for hearing and answering your requests. Rejoice in your personal forgiveness through Christ.

Your prayer space:

CONCLUSION

Has my research, study, prayer, and writing for this project turned me into a role model of God-pleasing self-care? Not even close. But I am even more convinced of its value. With Holy Spirit infusion, I'll continue to pursue self-discipline and nurture. And like all behavioral changes, I can expect some relapse into familiar unhealthy habits, and the need to aggressively pursue motivation to get back on track.

My struggles have been shared in hopes of encouraging you to personalize this book's information. Have any of your answers to the introductory quiz in this book changed? What positives did you discover you were already doing? If you gained insight or encouragement while reading these chapters, join this author in *giving God glory.*

My prayer is for the Lord to guide you in obvious ways, as you seek to live out his will.

Want to help share this book's insights with others? Your review on Amazon, and your social media shares are appreciated! For information on how to use this book as a group study, contact the author at graceitforward@outlook.com.

ACKNOWLEDGMENTS

Unless noted, scripture quotation are from the Holy Bible, Evangelical Heritage Version ® (EHV ®) © 2017 Wartburg Project, Inc. All rights reserved. Used by permission. Clip arts are from Cliker.com.

I am indebted to the following for their contributions, prayers, and encouragement:

- Leah Alair
- Linda Buxa (editor/author)
- Robin Fry
- Lisa Gotshall
- Debra Graf (Graf Counseling)
- Elise Gross (WELS Kingdom Workers)
- Sarah Haben
- Jas Lonnquist Klebig (screenwriter, Writtenbyjas.com)
- Diane Kratz
- Carly Laabs (Theparachuteproject.com)
- Susan Ann Lueneburg (Susanannmusic.com)
- Darci Matzke
- Lisa Miller
- Jill Murtagh
- Mary Schmal (author, Childrenofthelightbooks.com)
- Pastors Mark Jeske, Daron Lindemann, Mike Novotny, Jared Natsis, Tom Pankow, and Dean Zemple
- Sharon Steinfest
- Brandon Steenbock (staff minister, St. Mark De Pere)
- Greg Schmill (Grace in Action)
- Amber Albee Swenson (author, Amberalbeesweson.com)
- Arlyss Troge
- Keith Wakeman
- Jess Woller (author, *A Miraculous Debut*)

APPENDIX

Self-Care Quiz

Answering the following questions will help you find personalized ways to do self-care.

1. WHAT GIVES ME EMOTIONAL ENERGY?

2. WHAT MAKES ME LAUGH?

3. WHAT ADDS JOY TO MY DAYS?

4. WHAT HELPS ME SLEEP PEACEFULLY?

5. WHAT ASSISTS MY DECISION-MAKING?

6. WHICH ACTIVITIES/OPPORTUNITIES ARE THE MOST BEN-
   EFICIAL FOR ME?

7. WHAT HABITS TEACH AWARENESS OF MY LIMITS?

8. WHEN DO I TRULY RELAX?

9. WHAT INFLUENCES ARE PERSONALLY REJUVENATING?

10. WHEN DO I FEEL MOST SECURE, OPTIMISTIC, OR
    GROUNDED?

11. WHICH PEOPLE AND RELATIONSHIPS ARE SUPPORTIVE
    AND NURTURING FOR ME?

What's Your Self-Love Language?

Perhaps you have heard of Gary Chapman's book *The Five Love Languages*. Counselors at Christian Family Solutions took those concepts and applied them to self-care. Which of the following might you prefer to encourage yourself toward healthy habits?

Affirmation. Use positive self-talk. Write an affirmation. Journal your strengths. Identify favorite traits. Note compliments from people.

Acts of Service. Keep a calendar. Plan your meals. Schedule well visits. Clean your environment. Simplify with auto-pay, grocery delivery, etc.

Quality Time. Limit your commitments. Take time for hobbies. Detox from social media. Make plans with friends. Schedule time for self-care every week.

Physical Touch. Get a massage. Take a long, hot bath. Snuggle in a blanket. Stretch your muscles. Moisturize your skin with lotion or oils.

Receiving Gifts. Treat yourself to lunch. Buy one thing you love. Invest in your dreams. Plan a vacation. Complete one bucket list experience.

(Reprinted with permission from WLCFS-Christian Family Solutions, christianfamilysolutions.org, info@wlcfs.org)

Power Verses

The devil hates those who are prepared for his assaults. It may not be in style to wear armor, but it is required for spiritual warfare and faith protection (Ephesians 6:10–17). Memorizing the Word of God is an effective way to strike Satan with "the sword of the spirit" to chase him out of your life.

Read, reread aloud, write out, sing, and memorize:

> May your whole spirit, soul, and body be kept blameless at the coming of our Lord Jesus Christ. The one who calls you is faithful, and he will do it. (1 Thessalonians 5:23–24)

> This is the reason I have hope: By the mercies of the LORD we are not consumed, for his compassions do not fail. They are new every morning. Great is your faithfulness. (Lamentations 3:21–23)

> So then, there is now no condemnation for those who are in Christ Jesus. For in Christ Jesus the law of the Spirit of life set me free from the law of sin and death. (Romans 8:1–2)

> He chose us in Christ before the foundation of the world, so that we would be holy and blameless in his sight. (Ephesians 1:4)

Spiritual Nurture

> Let the word of Christ dwell in you richly, as you teach and admonish one another with all wisdom, singing psalms, hymns,

and spiritual songs, with gratitude in your hearts to God. (Colossians 3:16)

Let us hold on firmly to the confession of our hope without wavering, since he who promised is faithful. (Hebrews 10:23)

Indeed, whatever was written in the past was written for our instruction, so that, through patient endurance and the encouragement of the Scriptures, we would have hope. (Romans 15:4)

Emotional/Mental Nurture

Whatever is true, whatever is honorable, whatever is right, whatever is pure, whatever is lovely, whatever is commendable, if anything is excellent, and if anything is praiseworthy, think about these things. (Philippians 4:8)

The Lord is your teacher. Whenever you are tempted to turn to the right or to the left, you will hear his voice behind you, saying, "This is the way. Walk in it." (Isaiah 33:20–21)

Rejoice always. Pray without ceasing. In everything give thanks. For this is God's will for you in Christ Jesus. (1 Thessalonians 5:16–18)

Therefore, as God's elect, holy and loved, clothe yourselves with heartfelt compassion, kindness, humility, gentleness, and patience. (Colossians 3:12)

Physical Nurture

So whether you eat or drink, or do anything else, do everything to the glory of God. (1 Corinthians 10:31)

She wraps strength around her waist like a belt, and she makes her arms strong. (Proverbs 31:17)

He is the one who gives strength to the weak, and he increases the strength of those who lack power. (Isaiah 40:29)

Social/Relationship Nurture

Therefore, encourage one another and build each other up, just as you are also doing. (1 Thessalonians 5:11)

Look, how good and how pleasant it is when brothers live together in unity! (Psalm 133:1)

Do not go along with someone who has a hot temper. If you do, you will learn his ways and set a trap for yourself. (Proverbs 22:24–25)

Whoever walks with the wise becomes wise, but a companion of fools suffers harm. (Proverbs 13:20)

ABOUT THE AUTHOR

Susan L. Fink is a frequent contributor to *Holy Hen House* magazine and their blog (Holyhenhouse.com) as well as her own "Reflection, Inspiration, and Humor" posts (Susanlfink.blogspot.com). She is the author of *How Christian Mothers Cope* and the e-book *Developing a Devoted Family: Reasons and Resources for Home Worship*. Susan's life experiences include teaching Sunday school, preschool, and high school; being a hospice volunteer coordinator and grief group facilitator; and being a wife and mother to three multitalented, grown children and one perfect granddaughter. A continual student of Scripture, her desire is to encourage others to seek and share the joy of "hearts burning within us" for Jesus and his Word.